REVELATIONS
OF WOMEN MYSTICS

revelations of women mystics

From the Middle Ages to Modern Times

by

José de Vinck

"All manner of things shall be well!"
Dame Julian of Norwich

ALBA · HOUSE   NEW · YORK

SOCIETY OF ST. PAUL, 2187 VICTORY BLVD., STATEN ISLAND, NEW YORK 10314

Library of Congress Cataloging in Publication Data

De Vinck, José, 1912
 Revelations of women mystics.

 Bibliography: p.
 Includes index.
  1. Private revelations.   2. Women mystics.
 I. Title.
 BV5091.R4D48   1985   248.2'2   84-24485
 ISBN 0-8189-0478-X

*Designed, printed and bound in the United States of
America by the Fathers and Brothers of the
Society of St. Paul, 2187 Victory Boulevard,
Staten Island, New York 10314, as part of their
communications apostolate.*

2 3 4 5 6 7 8 9 (Current Printing: first digit).

To Mary the Mother of God
Rosa Mystica, ora pro nobis!

CONTENTS

INTRODUCTION

We now live in the age of science. Its effects, good and bad, are all around us, from the marvelous benefits of technology to its threat of utter destruction. We also live in the age of scientists, some of whom believe everything will be explained ultimately by the mechanical laws of materialistic determinism. Others, by contrast, on reaching the top of the mountain of knowledge, are delighted to discover theologians and mystics who have reached it before them by entirely different paths. The scientific vision of the universe, attained through inductive experimentation, coincides surprisingly with the discoveries of men and women of all ages who seem to have flown to the summits on the wings of intuitive grace.

At the highest point of every investigation, scientist and believer alike are baffled by mystery. What had seemed to be the highest peak turns out to be merely the topmost point attainable by human intelligence. The true summit is elsewhere, totally out of reach. And so, all investigators of Truth are faced with the choice between Satan's refusal to bow and Mary's trusting consent: they may either stand in pride, or kneel in adoration before the sacred, the numinous, the entirely Other, the mystery of some Reality more intimately subjective than their own selves, and yet totally beyond it.

Napoleon Bonaparte, at the height of his power, boasted that the future was his. He was immediately put down by the chaplain to whom he spoke: "The future, Sire, belongs to no one: the future is God's!" If it were not, there would be very little hope for our messed-up world. Yet, although the future is in God's hands, he combines his supreme authority with human freedom: man will be left to blunder and bleed, to exterminate millions of his own kind under the pretext of purifying the race, of expanding national territory, or simply for the sake of grabbing for his own selfish use as much as possible of the limited goods of the earth.

In spite of all the tragedies of history, there is however in the human psyche a deep faith in the ultimate power of Love and a belief that in the end — as Julian of Norwich put it — ''All manner of things shall be well.''

The scriptural foundation for this optimistic view is a text from 1 Corinthians 2:9 (quoting Isaiah): ''What no eye has seen nor ear heard nor the heart of man conceived, what God has prepared for those who fear him, God has revealed to us through the Spirit.'' The prophets of this faith are the mystics, a group of highly privileged individuals who serve as the means of communication between God and mankind. Mystical favors are shared equally between men and women — and many of the very greatest mystics are women.

Before going any further, it may be good to clarify the notion of ''mystic.'' The term has been applied to the ancient Greek mysteries of Eleusis and to many forms of personal relationship with the divine. In various loose and weakened senses, the words ''mystic'' and ''mystical'' have come to mean 'baffling,' 'enigmatic,' 'obscure,' 'mystifying,' 'vague,' 'inducing a feeling of awe,' or 'having magical properties.' They have even been used commercially, as in ''mystic tape'' and geographically, as in Mystic, Connecticut, although this seems much more simply to have an Indian derivation.

The adjective ''mystical'' as defined by Noah Webster comes close to our topic: ''Having a spiritual meaning, existence, reality or the like, neither apparent to the senses nor obvious to the intelligence.''

With such a variety of possible meanings, it is no wonder that the words "mystic" and "mystical" and anything related to them will tend to make people wary.

The most common misconception is that mystical experience is an illusion, a superstition of the ignorant. Many a sophisticated philosopher refuses even to look into such matters. In fact, the historical and literary confirmations of true mystical phenomena are so overwhelming as to make the skeptic seem ignorant and superstitious.

There is a deep reason that keeps people — even good people, priests and religious included — at a safe distance from any mystical contact: a very real sense of fear. Some manifestations of mysticism are so awesome as to remind us of the biblical saying: "It is a fearful thing to fall into the hands of the Living God!" (Heb 10:31). Mystical involvement, when it reaches the depths attained by a Saint John of the Cross, the two Theresas and, as we shall see, a Sister Josefa Menéndez, implies such an abyss of self-denial, such a total sacrifice of human values, that very few are able to consider it in others, let alone practice it in themselves. And so, out of a sense of prudence, excusable yet imperfect, many good people shun even indirect contact with the existential reality of the Living God.

Others, by contrast, are irresistibly attracted by it, perhaps more so in our times than ever before because of the urgent necessity of finding a better foundation for life than that offered by materialistic technology. The young are going on an all-out search for real and permanent values, for something to which, or to whom, to devote their energy and idealism. Often, unfortunately, they seem to be giving too much attention to the "mystic" religions of the East. Many also indulge in strange messianic cults that exploit their gullibility while depriving them of any kind of personal thought. In exchange for their independence, and generally also for their money, they are offered a tightly-knit cocoon of false security, a kind of hypnotic servility to some guru who becomes immensely rich in the process. Besides these fads, however, there has always been a deep current of true mysticism that surfaces in every genuine investigation of the divine, in ways proper to local culture: among the early Egyptians and the Mayas, the Hindus and the Buddhists, the Persians and the Arabs — but most clearly and substantially in the Judeo-Christian tradition.

Because of the obvious good will of many searchers-for-God outside our own faith, an attempt was made to include in the present book the works of women mystics with different allegiances, many of whom have undoubtedly experienced personal contact with God. Letters indicating our purpose were addressed to authorities from Iran, India and Egypt and to several leaders in Orthodox, Protestant and Jewish communities. Unfortunately, not one pertinent response was ever received. The closest we ever got was to some Muslim sources — but these proved to be a dead-end because nothing seemed to have been published in the six or seven languages we could read. By necessity, then, the only women mystics studied here happen to be Roman Catholics. Their countries of origin are Germany, Belgium, Italy, England, Spain, Mexico, South Africa and France. Four of these women are ancient, belonging to the thirteenth and fourteenth centuries, and four are modern, from the nineteenth and twentieth. The chosen names do not include the greatest and better-known mystics whose works have been studied by others in great detail. Our selection comprises the following:

— Mechtild of Magdeburg (ca. 1207-1282)
— Hadewyck of Antwerp (ca. 1250)
— Angela of Foligno (1248-1309)
— Julian of Norwich (1342-?)
— Josefa Menéndez (1890-1923)
— Conchita (1862-1937)
— Louisa Jaques (1901-1942)
— Gabrielle Bossis (1874-1950)

Approaching any true mystical experience is like taking a deep dive into an unknown sea. The usual pattern of life must be left behind. Logic becomes useless. The sudden shock of the glowing and glittering world of the spiritual diver makes us lose all sense of ordinary reality, replacing it with another which in fact is much more real, although at times it may seem unbelievable and incomprehensible — even absurd — for the ways of God are not the ways of man. And this is particularly true in the depths of mysticism where the diver encounters marvels beyond description.

When the explorers of coral reefs come floating into the exquisite underwater world, their eyes are delighted by a constant variety of forms, colors and motions: brilliant red starfish, snow-white or salmon-pink corals, gaudy striped parrot fish, black spindly sea-urchins, delicate mauve sea-anemones waving their feather-like tendrils. The spectators of such marvels wish to share such pleasant sights, to pluck such marvels out of the deep and bring them back to the dry and brittle land of ordinary men. Alas, the scarlet star turns into a pinkish blob, the anemone into a graying ooze, the splendid fish into a gasping, dying victim of human curiosity.

The mystics are the divers of the spiritual sea. They, too, encounter marvels too bright to keep for themselves: they want to pluck them and share them with other people who do not have the slightest inkling of what is going on beneath the surface of life, but seem content with the dust of their own routine. Alas, as soon as the spiritual divers attempt to bring to the surface any of the marvels they have seen — as soon as they try to explain in human words the revelations of God's tender love — nothing is left but pale approximations in terms that are never able to convey the reality, the liveliness or the splendor of what had been perceived.

The sorrow of the mystics because of their inability to share what they have seen is a common theme of their complaints — whether they are using their own words, or are having them transcribed by a secretary. As we shall see, Angela of Foligno suffered from the inability of her faithful scribe to put down in sufficiently vivid Latin what she was describing to him in her Italian dialect.

It takes a rare coincidence to combine mystical and literary gifts, as occured in the outstanding case of Teresa of Avila. Most women mystics never came near her level of culture. In earlier instances, they were further handicapped by the sorry condition of the education of women. There are, then, many more true mystics than those whose works have come to us — many who have experienced the personal presence of God without recording it in literary form. Perhaps you will miss your favorite: if so, please forgive me and complete my too-limited knowledge of the field. Please also keep in mind that this book is no encyclopedia, but a florilegium, a collection of flowers gathered here for your pleasure and edification. May these examples of the writings of holy women inspire many readers to look into themselves and respond to the stirrings of the Spirit of Love.

I

MECHTILD OF MAGDEBURG

MECHTILD OF MAGDEBURG
(ca. 1207-1282)

No clear date can be determined for Mechtild of Magdeburg's birth or death. From the little she reveals in her own writings, and from data culled from the writings of her contemporaries and companions, St. Mechtild of Hackeborn and St. Gertrude the Great, she was born in Saxony some time between 1207 and 1210 and died in the Cistercian convent of Helfta some time between 1282 and 1294. Her parents were wealthy and belonged to the nobility. She must have been well educated, despite the fact that she denies it. Perhaps her denials refer to her lack of full training in the study of Scripture and the Fathers, by contrast with her sisters of the convent of Helfta, which she entered toward the end of her life. However, her knowledge of spiritual matters must have been precocious, since her first "greetings" by the Holy Spirit occurred when she was only twelve (cf. *"Overflowing Light of the Godhead,"* IV:2). When she was about twenty, she left her parents to follow the call of divine love and settled in "exile" in the relatively distant town of Magdeburg, where she remained for some thirteen years in a community of "beguines."

The "beguines" were widows and holy women, living together in loose-knit communities, often having their own little houses and private gardens, and devoting their lives to good works and worship. They were not bound by any religious vows, but constituted a kind of third-order within the Church. They flourished in southern Germany, and mostly in Flanders. Their "beguinages" — cottages grouped around a central court with a chapel, the whole surrounded by a wall, with a single arched door as an entrance — may still be seen in the museum-city of Bruges and in Louvain, both in Belgium.

For the longest time, Mechtild concealed the marvelous action of divine love upon her life. Only around 1250, and for the next thirty years of her life, did she consign her mystical experiences in writing by order of her Dominican confessor, Henry of Halle. This resulted in her extraordinary book, *Das fliessende Licht der Gottheit, The Overflowing Light of the Godhead*.

What seems characteristic of this Story of a Soul is the peaceful frankness with which she criticizes both the Empire and the Church, thus bringing upon herself much enmity and indignation, the intensity of which demonstrates the scope of her influence. Hounded by her enemies after she had denounced the vices of the clergy of her time, she was forced to seek refuge around 1270 in the Cistercian convent of Helfta, not far from Magdeburg. There, in an atmosphere of scholarship and deep spirituality, she found companions worthy of her high ideals. At one time, she joined the Dominican Order, and must have become Prioress, since in her later works, she writes about the duties of a Superior.

Henry of Halle had composed six books out of her writings. In Helfta, she added a seventh which she dictated when she became quite blind. She died with a reputation of holiness, but was never beatified or canonized.

The style of Mechtild's writing is often startling, because she came under the influence of the literary fashion of her time, that of the minnesingers or troubadours who exalted the romantic excesses of courtly love, attributing heroic travails to imaginary personages. In Mechtild's works, God often appears as the Emperor, Christ as the King, the heavenly choirs as the courtiers of heaven, and all of them speak in flowery terms of human love. Another of Mechtild's surprising themes is the inebriation of love, so that many of her poems sing the joys of the tavern and of strong drink, much to the consternation of puritans. She passes unexpectedly from prose into poetry, then back again to prose, according to her own inner rhythm.

Mechtild, in Part 4, Chapter 2 of her book *"The Overflowing Light of the Godhead,"* gives in her own words a short account of the development of her spiritual life.

All my life, before I began this book and before a single word of it had come from God into my soul, I was the simplest creature who ever appeared in the spiritual life. Of the devil's wickedness, I knew nothing, nor of the evil of the world; and of the falseness of so-called spiritual people I had no idea.

Now I must glorify God through speech as well as through the writing of this book. I, unworthy sinner, was greeted so overpoweringly by the Holy Spirit in my twelfth year when I was alone, that I could no longer have given way to any serious daily sin. The loving greeting came every day and caused me both love and sorrow; the sweetness and glory increased daily — and this continued for thirty-one years.

I knew nothing of God except the usual Christian beliefs, and I tried to follow them diligently that my heart might become pure. God is my witness that I never consciously asked him to give me the things of which I have written in this book. I had never dreamt that such things could come to any human being. While I lived with relatives and friends to whom I was most dear, I had no inkling of such matters. But I had for long wished to be despised . . . .

Then through the love of God I went to a town (Magdeburg) where I had no friends save only one. I feared that through the latter my renunciation of the world and my love of God might be interfered with. But God never left me. He brought me such sweetness of love, such heavenly knowledge, such inconceivable wonders, that I had little use

for earthly things. Then was my spirit first brought out of my
prayer and set between heaven and earth. And I saw with the
eyes of my soul in heavenly bliss, the beautiful humanity of
Our Lord Jesus Christ and I knew him by his shining countenance. I saw the Holy Trinity, the eternity of the Father, the
work of the Son and the sweetness of the Holy Spirit.

Such a modest confession reveals to us, among other things,
that the young child of twelve was already well advanced on the
way to holiness, since she "wished to be despised," undoubtedly
in conformity with what she had learned about Christ. The soil of
her soul had been well prepared for a rich spiritual flowering, even
if it did come to her as a surprise. Once again, as so often happened
in the annals of spiritual favors, Christ revealed himself intimately
to one of his little ones. She is surprised, and relates this delightful
conversation with the Lord:

> "Ah! Lord! were I a learned priest
> and hadst thou worked this wonder in him,
> then hadst thou endless honor therefrom.
> "But how can any believe
> that on this unworthy soil
> thou couldst raise up a golden house
> and live therein with thy Mother
> and all creatures,
> and all the heavenly host.
> "Lord! therein can I find no earthly wisdom!"
> "Daughter! many a wise man loses his precious gold
> carelessly on the great highway
> on which he would come to the upper school;
> but some must find it!
> I have long acted thus:
> Wherever I gave special grace,
> I sought for the lowest and smallest and most hidden.
> The highest mountains may not receive

the revelations of my grace,
for the flood of my Holy Spirit
flows by nature down into the valleys.
   "One finds many a writer of books
who in himself, to my sight, is a fool,
and I tell thee further: it greatly honors me
and strengthens mightily Holy Church
that unlearned lips should teach
the learned tongues of my Holy Spirit" (*Ibid.*, II:26).

Even after hearing such kindly words, Mechtild had doubts
concerning the value of her work, and was in great need of
reassurance:

   I was warned about this book and told by many
   that it should not be preserved
   but rather thrown to the flames.
      Then did I what from childhood I have done
   when trouble overcame me:
   I betook myself to prayer;
   I bowed to my Love and said:
   "Lord! now I am troubled!
   Must I walk uncomforted for thy glory?
   Thou hast misled me
   for thou thyself commandest me to write."
      Then God showed himself to my weary soul,
   and holding the Book in his right hand, he said:
   "Beloved! fret not thyself too sore!
   The truth may no man burn.
   Those who would take this book out of my hand
   must be stronger than I!
   This book is threefold
   and concerns me alone . . . .
   Now, see in all these words

how praisefully they proclaim my holiness
and doubt not thyself.''

And so, Mechtild continued to confide her revelations to her notebooks, writing them in a Low-German dialect which was later translated into Latin by Henry of Halle, and into High-German by Henry of Nordlingen. The original text is lost: only the two translations survived.

The value of *Fliessende Licht* is both spiritual and literary. Mechtild is able to express in lyrical fashion the sorrows and delights of her mystical experience, to compose dialogues between God and the soul, between the soul and the conscience or the devil, all this with such taste and talent that one of her translators, Henry of Nordlingen, confessed in 1345: "It is the most marvelous German, and the fruit of the most appeasing love I have ever read in the language" (*Letter 43*).

The major point of Mechtild's doctrine seems to be the passionate assertion, based on her mystical experience, of the fact that she belonged to God by nature. Not only does she affirm that her writings come "from the living Godhead spilled in her heart" (VI: 43), but she seeks many times to express by means of repetition the sweetness of the connatural union with God which transports her body and senses.

"God has granted to all creatures
That they live according to their nature.
How could I, then, oppose my nurture?
Far from all else, I must give myself to God
Who is my Father by nature,
My Brother through humanity,
My Betrothed in love."
"And I, who am his without beginning,
Do you think I could not feel that nature? . . . .
Spouse-soul, you must be so well 'ennatured' in me
That nothing could exist between you and me" (I: 44).

His divinity is never foreign to me,
For always and without any fetters,
I feel it in every one of my limbs (II: 12).

God flows into her "like a springing and bottomless fountain" (I: 8), and declares to her: "Between you and me, there is the constant exchange of an inconceivable breath" (II: 24). Through the symbols of sparkling light, heat and fire, Mechtild shows how the soul's desire meets that of God. The soul "ran out originally from God's heart, and must needs return there" (V: 22). She could not be content with the light of angels, for her essence is "noble desire and unquenchable avidity" (I: 44).

Another important aspect of Mechtild's writing is a trinitarian bent. Her many experiences of love are developed within a threefold mystery. "God the Father is the Vintner of this inebriating life, the Son is the Cup, the Spirit is the Wine" (II: 24). She asks for no favors, but God begs of her: "Grant that I may refresh in you the burning embers of my Godhead, the desire of my Humanity and the joy of my Holy Spirit" (IV: 2). Her experience of love in the spiritual wedding is expressed in a trinitarian way:

Let him [Christ] open to me the joyful flow
that runs within the Holy Trinity,
the soul's only source of life. . . .
For the blissful Sun of the living Godhead
shines through the pure water of happy Humanity,
and the sweet joy of the Holy Spirit
proceeds from the one and from the other (IV: 12).

There are throughout Mechtild's writings many more references to this trinitarian theology. In this, her doctrine resembles closely that of one of her contemporaries, the Prince of Mystics, St. Bonaventure of Bagnorea. Other influences are clear, in spite of Mechtild's originality. Besides St. Bonaventure, she must have been familiar with St. Gregory the Great, William of St. Thierry

and the Victorines, and particularly with the Pseudo-Dionysius.
Her views on the relationship between the natural and the
supernatural are close to those of Thomas Aquinas. All in all,
however, she seems to go well beyond Scholastic intellectualism
by placing faith — the night of the spirit and the total unknowing of
love — far ahead of any dogmatic teaching.

> "Your mountain shall be melted away by love,
> your enemies shall win no victories over you;
> your acre has been scorched by a hot sun,
> yet its fruit has not been destroyed.
> In my Kingdom, you shall live as a new bride:
> there will I kiss you with a kiss of love
> and all my Godhead shall sweep through your soul.
> My threefold vision shall play ceaselessly
> in your twofold heart" (IV: 5).
> Lord and heavenly Father, you are my heart.
> Lord Jesus Christ, you are my body.
> Lord Holy Spirit, you are my breath.
> Lord Holy Trinity, you are my only refuge
> and my everlasting peace (V: 6).

This short invocation could serve as the basis for deep meditation. It could also serve as a daily prayer for anyone who wishes to
live in the presence of God.

As so often happens in Mechtild's writings, poems alternate
with prose with no other apparent reason than the mood of the
moment. One of the most moving passages is related to the Trinity:

> The true greeting of God, which comes from the heavenly
> flood out of the spring of the flowing Trinity, has such power
> that it takes all strength from the body and lays the soul bare to
> itself. Thus it sees itself as one of the blessed and receives in
> itself divine glory. The soul is then separated from the body,
> with its power and love and longing. Only the smallest part of

life remains to the body, which is as it were in a sweet sleep. The soul sees God as One and Undivided in Three Persons, and the Three Persons in One Undivided God. God greets the soul in the language of the court of heaven not understood in this kitchen (the earthly world). And he clothes it with such garments as are worn in his palace and girds it with strength. Then it may ask what it will, and that shall be granted.

Should it not be granted, it is because the soul is taken further by God to a secret place where it must not ask nor pray for anyone, for God alone will play with it in a game of which the body knows nothing, any more than the peasant at the plough or the knight in the tourney — not even his loving Mother Mary: she can do nothing here. Thus God and the soul soar further to a blissful place of which I neither can nor will say much: it is too great and I dare not speak of it, for I am a sinful creature.

Moreover, when the infinite God brings the unmoored soul up into the heights of contemplation, it loses touch with the earth in face of that wonder, and forgets it ever was upon the earth. When this flight is at its height, the soul must leave it. Then the All-Glorious God speaks: "Maiden! thou must humble thyself and descend again."

She is affrighted, and says: "Lord! thou hast drawn me up so high that I am out of myself and cannot praise thee with any order in my body, for I suffer grievously and strive against my body."

Then he speaks: "Ah! my dove! thy voice is music to my ears, thy words are as savor to my mouth, thy longing as the gentleness of my gifts."

And she replies: "Dear Lord! all must be as the Master ordains."

And she sighs so deeply that her body is awakened and asks: "Lady, where hast thou been? Thou comest so lovingly back, so beautiful and strong, so free and full of spirit! But thy wanderings have taken from me my zest, my peace, my color, all my powers.''

The soul exclaims: ''Silence! Destroyer! Cease thy complaints! I will ever guard myself against thee. That my enemy should be wounded does not trouble me, I am glad of it.''

That Mechtild should see her body as her enemy is very much in the spiritual style of her time. St. Bernard and many others pushed the dualism of body and soul to a level approaching Manicheism. It is only in the spirituality of Francis of Assisi that ''Brother Body'' begins to receive his humble due.

Another characteristic of the spirituality of the time is an attempt to reach salvation through flight from the world. Mechtild refers to it, but in practice, through her own good works as a beguine and her deep concern with the reformation of the Church of her time, she remains very much in the world, and certainly gains more merit from this fact than from any idealistic attempt to escape from reality.

There comes now a moving poem on a theme often found in religious poetry, the Love Chase, best known through Francis Thompson's *The Hound of Heaven:*

I:3   THE SOUL

> ''Ah, dearest Love, for how long
> hast thou lain in wait for me!
> What, oh what can I do?
> I am hunted, captured, bound,
> wounded so terribly
> that never can I be healed.
> Cunning blows hast thou dealt:
> shall I ever recover from thee?
> Would it not have been well
> that I had never known thee?''

LOVE

"I hunted thee for my pleasure,
I caught thee for my desire,
I bound thee for my joy:
Thy wounds have made us one,
my cunning blows me thine.
I drove Almighty God
from heaven, and it was I
who took his human life
and gave him back again
with honor to his Father.
How couldst thou hope, poor worm,
to save thyself from me?"

THE SOUL

"But Queen, I fear I might
through one small gift of God,
through food and drink, escape thee?"

LOVE

"That prisoners may not die,
one gives them bread and water,
and God has given thee these,
mere respites for a time.
But when thy death-blow falls,
and when thy Easter comes,
I shall be all around thee,
I shall be through and through thee,
and I shall steal thy body
and give thee to thy Love."

THE SOUL

"Love! I have been thy scribe:
seal those words with thy sign."

LOVE

"Who loves God more than self
knows where to find the seal:
it lies between us twain.
The seal is there, thine Easter come,
and God, thy glorious grave, thy home."

A little later, there is a short poem deep with meaning:

I:21   Love without knowledge
is darkness to the wise soul.
Knowledge without revelation
is as the pain of hell.
Revelation without death
cannot be endured.

This is a sublime summary of the spiritual life. First, there is the natural hunger of the human heart expressing itself in the form of love seeking its object. As long as this object is not properly identified, the lover is groping in darkness. Then knowledge identifies the love-object as some form of absolute good, but as long as this absolute good takes any form besides God — be it wealth, or success, or power, or pleasure — it leads to the vacuum of hell, to the absence of the revealed God who is the true and proper object of total human love. But as soon as revelation has enlightened the lover, nothing on earth is sufficient to satisfy her love, and she realizes that death alone is the way to God.

I:33   My soul spake thus to her Love: "Lord! thy tenderness is a wonderful trust to my body, thy compassion an unspeakable comfort to my soul, thy love to my whole being rest eternal!"

And the Lord answers:

I:34   "Thou art my lamb in thy sufferings,
my dove in thy sighings,
my bride in thy watching."

In a delightful series of animal-symbols, God rejoices because the soul has overcome four sins:

I:38   "Look how she who wounded me has risen!
      She has cast from her the apes of worldliness,
      overcome the bear of impurity,
      trodden the lion of pride underfoot,
      torn the wolf of desire from his revenge,
      and comes racing like a hunted deer
      to the spring which is Myself.
      She comes soaring like an eagle
      swinging herself from the depths
      up unto the heights."

Then the theme of the Love-Chase is resumed, God asking the soul what she can offer him.

I:39-43   GOD

    "Thou huntest sore for thy love:
    what bring'st thou me, my queen?"

      THE SOUL

    "Lord! I bring thee my treasure:
    it is greater than the mountains,
    wider than the world,
    deeper than the sea,
    higher than the clouds,
    more glorious than the sun,
    more manifold than the stars.
    It outweighs the whole earth."

        GOD

    "O thou! image of my divine Godhead,
    ennobled by my humanity,

adorned by my Holy Spirit,
what is thy treasure called?''

THE SOUL

''Lord! it is called my heart's desire.
I have withdrawn it from the world,
denied it to myself and all creatures.
Now I can bear it no longer:
where, O Lord, shall I lay it?''

GOD

''Thy heart's desire shalt thou lay nowhere
but in my divine Heart
and on my human breast.
There alone wilt thou find comfort
and be embraced by my Spirit. . . ''

I:44   THE SOUL

''Fish cannot drown in water,
birds cannot sink in the air,
gold cannot perish
in the refiner's fire.
This has God given to all creatures:
to foster and seek their own nature.
How then can I withstand mine?
I must to God —
my Father through nature,
my Brother through humanity,
my Bridegroom through love.
His am I forever.
''Think ye that fire
must utterly slay my soul?
Nay! Love can both fiercely scorch

and tenderly cherish and console.
Therefore be not troubled.''

I:6   GOD

"When I shine, thou must reflect,
when I flow, thou must race;
when thou sighest, thou dost draw
my divine Heart unto thee;
when thou weepest for me,
I take thee in my arms;
but when thou lovest me,
then are we twain one —
for thus united, nothing can separate us:
rather, a blissful waiting lies between us.''

THE SOUL

"Then, O Lord, I will wait with hunger and thirst,
eagerness and delight until that joyful hour
when the chosen words shall flow
from thy divine lips —
words which can be heard of none
save that soul alone which cuts itself loose
from the world to listen
to the words of thy mouth.
Such a soul alone can receive the Fount of Love.''

A little later, there comes a moving dialogue between the soul
and her desire:

III:1   The soul spake this to her desire:
"Fare forth and see where my Love is;
say to him that I desire to love.''
So desire sped forth,
for it is by nature swift,
and came to the Empyrean and cried,

"Great Lord, open, and let me in!"
Then said the Lord of that place:
"What means this fiery eagerness?"
"Lord! I would have thee know
that my lady can no longer live thus.
If thou wouldst flow forth to her,
then might she soar;
but the fish cannot live for long
stranded on the shore."
"Go back," said the Lord,
"I cannot let thee in
unless thou bring me that hungry soul
who alone delights me above all things."
As the messenger returned
and the soul perceived the will of her Lord,
ah! how lovingly she received it
and raised herself up in strong and happy flight!

Throughout all this romantic literature, there shines forth a genuine and glowing love, expressed with a rare and imaginative talent that places Mechtild among the great writers of her time. Yet, she maintains her unassuming humility:

III:1   Of the heavenly things God has shown me,
        I can speak but a little word,
        no more than a honey-bee
        can carry away on its foot.

There follows later in the same third part a moving analysis of the seeming conflict between God's compassion and his righteousness, so eloquently expressed in more recent times by the French writer Charles Péguy.

III:22   I have seen and heard of such boundless compassion of
        God that I asked: "Lord, how may that be?
        If thy righteousness companions thy compassion,

how is thy mercy so great?''
Then the Lord spoke a true word thus:
''I say to thee by my divine fidelity
that there are more in Holy Church
who go straight to heaven
than go down to hell.
For righteousness has its constant power
even if stained by sin,
and that I will never take from it,
for I come first of all as Father
to the burdened soul.
If I have had to take something good from it,
that comes from the great temptation
I suffer through my children.''
Then the soul spoke:
''Tell me, Lord, of thy temptation
that thy desire and mine may be made one.''
Our Lord said:
''Now hear how I am tempted:
My goodness and gentleness,
my faithfulness and compassion
force me so sore that I let them flow
over the mountains of pride,
the valleys of humility,
the thickets of disunity
and the smooth ways of purity.
But my mercy forces me yet further
than the ill will of wicked men forces them,
and my righteousness is greater
than all the wickedness of the devil.''
Then the soul spoke:
''Lord! thy righteousness
leads thee straight into the living Truth
and gives me joy unspeakable — without sorrow —

for wherever righteousness enters in,
truth rejoices.''

These are important words of consolation and reassurance for the many, taught by fearful and negative theologians who led them to believe that hell was overcrowded and heaven almost bare. The path to heaven may be narrow and the mouth of hell gaping wide, but God's righteousness tempered by his compassion is more powerful than all the devil's wiles.

The Lord continues with promises of love and joy:

IV:5   ''Thy mountains shall be melted away by love,
thine enemies shall win no victories over thee.
Thine acre has been scorched by a hot sun,
yet its fruit has not been destroyed.
In my kingdom thou shalt live as a new bride:
there will I kiss thee with a kiss of love
and all my Godhead shall sweep through thy soul.
My three-fold vision shall play ceaselessly
in thy two-fold heart.
Where, then, is now thy mourning?
If thou shouldst pray for a thousand years,
I would never give you cause for a single sigh.''

V:6   (The soul responds)
''Lord and heavenly Father, thou art my heart!
Lord Jesus Christ, thou art my body!
Lord Holy Spirit, thou art my breath!
Lord Holy Trinity, thou art my only refuge
and my everlasting peace!''

V:7   (Then the Lord)
''Thou art a foundation of my divine being
an honor of maidenly constancy,
a flower of great delight,

a vanquisher of evil spirits,
a mirror of eternal contemplation!''

VI:13   ''My Godhead came to earth,
my humanity accomplished the work;
my Godhead went to the cross,
my humanity suffered death;
my Godhead rose from death
and led humanity into heaven.
All who drive me from them
shall be driven from me.''

God's righteousness is infinite, and his mercy boundless, yet he is also all Justice and he lets man free to accept him or reject him. He extends that freedom to the point of granting the final wish of every soul. If that final wish is rejection, what the soul will get is the absence of God, which is another name for hell.

Throughout her life, Mechtild manifested a deep devotion to the Mother of God. During her very last years, when she was extremely weak and totally blind, she managed to dictate to her sisters the beautiful *Greetings to Our Lady in the Form of a Litany.*

VII:19   I greet thee, Lady, beloved Mary, that thou art
a joy to the Holy Trinity
the beginning of all our blessedness,
the companion of the holy angels
here and in the kingdom of God.

I greet thee, Lady, beloved Mary, that thou art
a flower of the patriarchs,
a hope of the prophets,
a white lily of humble maids.
Remember how the salutation of the Angel Gabriel
came to thee! And greet my soul on the last day,
and bring me with unclouded joy
out of this misery to the happy land

of thy dear Child,
that there I may find rest.

I greet thee, Lady, beloved Mary, that thou art
a wise teacher for the apostles,
a rose of the martyrs,
a gift of confessors,
a helper of widows,
an honor of all the saints of thy dear Child.
Pray for me that I in all my doings
be sanctified so far as may be
for me unworthy, Mary beloved Queen!

I greet thee, Lady, beloved Mary, that thou art
a refuge for sinners,
a strong helper for the perplexed,
a comforter to Holy Church,
a dread to evil spirits
who are driven away before thee.
Drive them also far from me
that they may never delight in me,
but that I may ever be constant
in thy service.

Even in her old age, Mechtild maintains her original humility:

VII:21   You ask teachings from me when I
           myself am unlearned!
           What you desire you will find a thousandfold in your books.

One of Mechtild's final writings touches with great depth upon the mystery of suffering:

VII:56   When man has sorrow
           of which he does not know the cause
           and yet is aware of little sin,

our Lord says to him:
"I have touched thee
in the same way in which
my Father let me be touched on earth.
In those I there draw to myself,
that causes much suffering,
but my friends should know truly
that the more I draw them,
the nearer they come to me.
When man makes a conquest over self,
so that suffering and consolation weigh equally,
then will I raise him to blessedness
and let him taste eternal life."

No more fitting conclusion could be found for the writing of
this great little one.

II

HADEWYCK OF ANTWERP

HADEWYCK OF ANTWERP
(ca. 1250)

Hadewyck of Antwerp was born in the first half of the thirteenth century. She is believed to have assumed the spiritual direction of a religious community of women. Her written work, in early Flemish, consists of fourteen *Visions,* many letters and a collection of rhymed poems published for the first time in 1875. A critical edition was issued in 1908/1914 under the direction of a Belgian priest, Father Van Mierlo. The poetical excerpts that follow are an original translation from this text. The excerpts from the letters are based on a French language version published by the Editions de la Phalange, Brussels (no date).

Hadewyck experiences the doubts and joys, the trials and rewards of the mystical life through alternating periods of absence and presence of God in her soul. She is also a keen observer of these phenomena, and analyzes her reactions to them with the depth of perception of a psychologist.

The first poem offered here, *Time Is New with Every Year,* is a general description of mystical love. The opening image is of the end of winter and the return of light, compared with the soul's hope for love. Once love has been attained, there is a two-fold reaction: hungering for more, and satiation — because the gift is so overwhelming it cannot be contained. Yet, in spite of all the pain, there comes a point where "man has nothing left but his faith in this high love." And Hadewyck advises total renewal of self in order to attain the everlasting newness of mystical love.

Time Is New With Every Year

Time is new with every year:
days of darkness become light.
Seeking love while lacking it,
oh, the wonder of such hope!

This new year is coming in!
For the man who turns his mind,
through some effort great or small
toward love, his grief is gain.

One who loves, yet spares the pain,
and so shows his lowliness,
wraps himself in stolen joys:
Rightly shall he feel their weight.

Those who come to life from love
and are nature's chosen ones
spare no toil for such a goal:
They will live in saintly warmth.

One who reaches love's high mount
he it is who welcomes pain,
for he looks upon his work
knowing well it has no end.

Shame upon the finer heart
which, by outer pressure duped,
fails to do the higher deed
that will keep its hunger keen.

Craving, sating — both in one —
such is the reward of love
as it may be seen by those
who consort in truth with it.

Craving:"Come, O Love supreme."
Sating: "Stop!" Such is the moan
for its light becomes too bright
and its blows turn into joy.

How can Love be deemed enough?
Oh, the marvel, it is he
who bestows his highest self
and imparts his treasured wealth.

How can hunger sustain love?
When a man knows he cannot
consummate what he desires,
this makes hunger stronger still.

How can light of love be pain?
When we cannot stand its gifts.
Nothing will compare with it
since it has no base in time.

Pleasures are but joust and strife
of true love by night and day,
since a man has nothing left
but his faith in this high love.

Holy Love I recommend
to all those who look for it.
For this goal, spare not your pains,
but comform your life with it.

Perhaps the most striking feature of Hadewyck's writing is her awareness of the dangers and ambivalences of the mystical life. Contemplation, for her, is not a safe and pleasurable bed of roses; rather, it is an arduous ascent through doubts and trials, often beyond logic or reason. This appears most clearly in the next poem:

The sweetest part of love is found in its assaults.
Its deepest abyss shines as its most splendid form.
Becoming lost in it is reaching to its core.
Starving to death for it is most delicious food.
Its total sense of loss is full security.
Its most severe wounds are means of perfect health.
Being consumed by it is everlasting life.
Hiding away from it is finding it anew.
Breaking one's heart for it is perfect sanity.
The healing it provides is challenge to the soul.
The losses it entails are its most lavish gifts.

There is no sense at all to its most splendid songs.
Imprisonment in it is total freedom found.
Its most appalling blows are its most tender boon.
Its total abstinence procures the richest gain.
Fleeing from it results in coming close to it.
Its low and humble silence is the most lofty song.
Its strongest wrath is but a cause for gratitude.
Its direst threats reveal the roots of faithfulness.
Its sorrow is the price it has to pay for joy.

And this too we can say when speaking about love:
Its wealth is nothing more than lack of everything.
The greatest trust in it may lead to sinking depths.
Its most essential form may cause a man to drown.
The fullness of its wealth may end in poverty.
Receiving much from it may lead to total loss.
Its consolations make for more severe wounds.
Its company has meant the death of quite a few.
Its food will make us starve; its knowledge is deceit.
What looks like wisdom is seduction at its hands.
Keep company with it, and you will suffer blows.
Its everlasting rest is always out of reach.

Attempts to make it seen will only hide it more.
The offering it makes is but a stolen gift.
Its promises are but deception unalloyed.
The garments it provides are nothing but undress.
Its messages of truth are but a bunch of lies.
Its total certainty is nothing but a fraud.

Such witnesses can I, and many others too,
confirm in all good faith at any time of day
since all too often Love has made it very plain
that what it had us do became a cause of scorn.
We only dreamed we had the gifts it kept ungiven.
And since the first appeal it made to my good will,
when I discovered how it was outwitting me,
I had to change the way I would behave with it.
As often by its threats as by its promises,
I was truly deceived and handled like a fool.
And yet, in spite of all, I want to be possessed,
for be it good or bad, all is the same for me.

The poem is divided into two major parts, separated by the line,
"And this too we can say when speaking about love." In the first
part, seemingly negative aspects of the mystical search are transformed into positive values through a series of paradoxical opposites that are reconciled in the encounter with God. This corresponds with traditional teachings. What is much more original
and mystifying is the second part which contains a reverse of the
first: Positive aspects of the contemplative life are shown to have
negative implications so powerful they seem to destroy what had
been said at first, and to leave the reader with serious doubts as to
the value of the experience. However, a careful analysis of the pairs
of opposites reveals a profound justification, a logical and
psychological truth. We will now consider in turn each line of the
second part:

1.   "The greatest trust in it may lead to sinking depths."

When supernatural love is used as a crutch, as a means of support and strengthening of temporal values, the spirit, instead of being lifted up to the vision of God, is cast down into the abyss, because love has been abused by its improper goal.

2.   "Its most essential form may cause a man to drown."

When such love of God and its response are perceived, and this gives rise to a sense of self-satisfaction because of the very height of the summits attained, there may be pride that leads to drowning.

3.   "The fullness of its wealth may end in poverty."

The excessive concentration on the joys imparted by mystical phenomena may be the cause of their cessation because of selfish concern.

4.   "Receiving much from it may lead to total loss.

The idea is the same as in the preceding line: the more joy one receives from intimacy with God, the more danger there is of losing everything through greed and excessive attachment.

5.   "Its consolations make for more severe wounds."

In this case, the wounds are not the result of any abuse, but of an ever-deepening involvement in the mystical life. The deeper this involvement, the greater the sorrow, because of an ever increasing hunger for the full possession of God. The "Dark Night of the Senses" — the absence of any feeling or emotional consolation — may be followed by the "Dark Night of the Spirit" — the loss of any intellectual certainty and the reduction to blind faith, a much more severe trial.

6.   "Its company has meant the death of quite a few."

Those who participate in the mystical revelations of love and use it merely for their own enjoyment, or for the prideful delectation of being "chosen" or "different," may fall into grievous and deadly sin, for the higher one has reached, the lower one is liable to fall.

7. *"Its food will make us starve."*

The supernatural quality of the experience of mysticism may be so violently appealing and satisfying that the more a mystic receives, the deeper the craving for the allness of God, which can never be attained.

8. *"Its knowledge is deceit."*

A mystic who believes she really understands what is going on is only fooling herself, since in that field any genuine experience is beyond rational understanding and interpretation.

9. *"What looks like wisdom is seduction at its hands."*

In their search for total supernatural wisdom, some mystics may fall for the seductive quality of the experience, seeking to satisfy some personal craving instead of offering themselves to God's love.

10. *"Keep company with it, and you will suffer blows."*

This, again, is a consequence of the mystical life itself, and not of its abuse. Total involvement in God's love will, by necessity, bring about hatred from the "world" — that is, from the unenlightened and all those under the influence of Satan — and will sometimes result in physical persecution by evil spirits, as in the case of John Vianney, or in violent death, as in the case of the martyrs.

11. *"Its everlasting rest is always out of reach."*

If a mystic starts out with the intention of reaching comfort and repose, she is sadly mistaken, since the exact oppo-

site will be given to her: hardships and labor, that is, participation
in the passion and cross of Christ.

   12.   "Attempts to make it seen will only hide it more."

The natural tendency of anyone who has gone through a true
mystical experience is to share with others its exalting moments —
but this is quite impossible since the experience is beyond words.
The more one tries to explain it, the more one falls into meaningless
babble, as occurred for instance in the case of Angela of Foligno
(See Chapter 3).

   13.   "The offering it makes is but a stolen gift."

Human beings are not entitled naturally to such high favors: in a
sense, they are "stolen" from heaven.

   14.   "Its promises are but deception unalloyed."

When a mystic pursues some personal benefit and believes she
has obtained some promise to that effect, such promise is vain since
it is imaginary. The true gifts of mysticism are gratuitous and
cannot be pursued.

   15.   "The garments it provides are nothing but undress."

Instead of offering material advantages (garments), the mystical life results in demanding that the subject give up everything —
an action the Greeks express with the word *Kenosis,* an emptying
out.

   16.   "Its messages of truth are but a bunch of lies."

Truth is in the rational, intellectual order. Mysticism goes
beyond reason, so that any attempt to understand and rationalize
the experience is doomed to failure.

17. *"Its total certainty is nothing but a fraud."*

In the mystical life, there is no plateau, no static achievement, no summit safe from fall where the soul is able to rest. On the contrary, the mystic is in a state of dynamic precariousness. She cannot stop and enjoy, but must go on and on through effort and vigilance until death.

Now, if we consider this line-by-line analysis, a pattern will appear. In some lines — 1, 2, 3, 4, 8, 9, 14, 16 — the negative aspects are consequences, not of the mystical experience itself, but of misinterpretations and misuse of it. In others — 5, 6, 7, 10, 11, 12, 13, 15 — the negative aspects are merely the price to be paid in order to reach the summit of divine love.

The first series, then, is not damaging to true mysticism, since it refers only to its possible distortions, while the second series faces the mystic with a judgment of values: is the goal worth the sacrifice?

Hadewyck reaches her own conclusion: beyond reason, beyond privation and suffering, she answers YES to the proposition of total surrender to the Spirit of God. Even the notion of good or bad, pleasure or pain, melts in the furnace of love:

"And yet, in spite of all, I want to be possessed,
For be it good or bad, all is the same for me."

The third selection is a development of Hadewyck's notion of life with God.

I would like to come close to true Love
if I could but attain to its core
— yet not one of those busy with things
will be able to join in my song.

Naked Love that will spare not a soul
in the treacherous passage of life
will be seen in its simplicity
at the time unessentials are crushed.

Let all those who surrender to Love
give up creatures and union with them:
Poor in spirit in the kingdom of earth,
they shall hold the new life as their due.

Nor is this to go traveling far,
nor to look for some bread or some good:
Poor in spirit, they give up chimeras
in the folds of a broad unity.

For a soul with no end or prelude,
with no form and no reason or sense,
with no model, no thought and no sign
has no circle to narrow it down.

In this madness of widening union
poor in spirit and living as one,
they will find in it nothing but leisure
that will give them eternal repose.

All of this may be said in few words,
but the passing is long, I know well,
for torments in great number befall
every soul that goes through to the end.

This whole poem may be transposed in a prose meditation that
goes something like this:

My dream is to come ever closer to God, my Lover, and
to reach the very center of his being. But I will be alone on this
journey, for none of those whose hearts are captured by
creatures will be able to come with me. Life is always

difficult, and at every step we are followed by God's love —
but only if we are able to give up the many vanities of the
world shall we see this love in its essential oneness. If, then,
we wish to offer ourselves entirely to God's love, let us give
up creature-comforts and our pursuit of them. Indeed, on
earth only the poor in spirit have a right to contemplative life.
Now, in order to succeed, we do not have to travel to distant
lands, nor should we seek contemplation as some kind of food
or treasure to be pursued selfishly: the poor in spirit make no
such mistake, for they are enfolded in God's oneness. If we
forget about past and future, if we give up every plan, every
rational argument, every desire; if we do without master,
thought or sign, we will escape from the prison of limitations.
In the seeming madness of total opening to union with God,
the poor in spirit cease to be obsessed with a thousand im-
mediate duties: They live the present day in full and begin to
enjoy eternal delight. Now, this is easily said in a few words,
but the road to union is long and arduous: I know it from
experience. Everyone who really takes the plunge into God
and decides to go all the way will have to suffer countless
torments in the course of his pilgrimage.

The mystical relationship between God and the soul is often
expressed by means of romantic — and even erotic — language, in
terms applying to the relationship between man and woman. This is
easy to understand, since human love is the deepest and most
personal form of contact available on the natural level. Now, since
all of our language and images are based on sense experience,
developed through imagination, and universalized in the form of
abstract words, it is only logical that these same words be applied to
a superhuman relationship that has no vocabulary of its own.
Hadewyck's letter IX is an example of this style of writing.

God, my dear child, gives you to understand what he is
and how he acts with men — and particularly with women —

who serve him. May he seize you within himself, for in the very place where the depth of his wisdom dwells, he will teach you who he is by making you know the ineffable bliss of lovers who enter each other and are so completely absorbed in each other that they are no longer able to distinguish their individual selves, but live the total fruitfulness of their love mouth to mouth, heart upon heart, body within body and soul within soul, while a gentle divine nature suffuses them entirely. And in this union of their selves, they yet remain themselves, and so do they go on forever.

III

ANGELA OF FOLIGNO

ANGELA OF FOLIGNO
(1248-1309)

A wooden statue of Angela of Foligno made when she was in her late thirties shows her as a short and slightly plump woman with a full-moon face. It is so life-like that it speaks clearly of her inner spirit: that of a lively woman, humorously enjoying the world and its pleasures, impulsive, willful, tending to be sarcastic and sharp-witted. She was living at the time with her mother, a frivolous woman who was doing her best to attract Angela to the ways of their local society. She also had a husband from whom she seems to have received little affection: in fact, there is no trace of anything he ever gave her besides several sons. She was then quite wealthy, concerned with fancy clothes and with the administration of a splendid domain that belonged to her personally.

Seized with remorse after several sacrilegious communions — following upon incomplete and insincere confessions — Angela prayed to St. Francis of Assisi, asking him for a confessor and for the grace of making a clean break with her worthless past. On the very same night, the saint assured her in a dream that her wish would be granted. Early next morning, she hastened to the cathedral of Assisi, where she came across a Franciscan friar— who happened to be a relative of hers — and made a full and satisfying confession, followed by the firm resolve to amend her way of life. The friar was Brother Arnaud, who was to become her official scribe, for as often happened in those days, Angela had never learned to write, although she was an educated woman who could read the Latin Missal.

Changing life in mid-course is a difficult enterprise for anyone. There followed four or five years of spiritual tribulations and hardships described in the first chapters of her writings. Her whole family died in short succession — mother, husband and sons. She gave up her fancy clothes and started selling all her possessions one by one, including her beautiful estate, the loss of which inflicted upon her a deep wound.

Some time in 1291, Angela decided to appeal once more to Saint Francis to help her achieve her goal. With a few companions, she again made the trip to Assisi. As soon as they arrived, they all went to the cathedral to pray for Angela's project, then they had lunch together. In the afternoon, Angela returned to the cathedral — but she fell on the threshold, uttering what sounded like meaningless cries. Her worried companions hastened to her side and gaped at her, not knowing what to do. The friars, attracted by the noise, came rushing out of the church — among them Brother Arnaud, humiliated and furious because she was making such a show of herself before the other friars, who all knew she was a relative of his. After she had regained her senses, he severely forbade her ever to come back to Assisi: he imagined she was suffering from epilepsy.

Yet, Brother Arnaud was curious, and his conscience bothered him. Some time later, as he was visiting Foligno, he called on his relative and entreated her to let him know the reason for her outcries. After some hesitation, she made him promise absolute secrecy and told him everything: On her way to Assisi, beyond Spello, at the junction of the road to Perugia and the path to Assisi, the Holy Trinity had revealed itself to her in a sensible way, and had spoken to her along the road and all the way into town, until she had reached the door of the cathedral for the second time. Then, as she suddenly perceived she was losing hold of the Supreme Good, she had fallen on the steps, trying in vain to cry out: "O Love Unknown, you cannot think of it! And why would you leave me in this way? Why, oh why, oh why?"

At this point, Arnaud sincerely believed his cousin to be possessed. He decided to make notes of everything he was witnessing in order to show them to experts of the spiritual life who would be able to discern under what kind of spirit Angela was acting. Finally convinced of the divine origin of her experience, he continued to take her dictation during five years, producing the first half of Angela's story, which could be called, "In Search of the Spirit." She was to have other secretaries later, but Arnaud was by far the most precise and the most conscientious.

Angela dictated rapidly; he could only write slowly. Angela told him about marvelous happenings he was unable to understand in full. He was forced to summarize — and she was deeply disappointed when her visions and revelations were read back to her in the flat and inexpressive language of every day.

Then, further trouble arose. The other friars, disturbed by Arnaud's constant presence at the side of a woman, began to spread scandalous rumours about him. His superior reprimanded him severely. He defended himself: "They did not know what I was writing, and what a good thing it was."

From 1296 until her death in 1309, others collected Angela's revelations. Their writings constitute the second half of her story. She dictated in an Italian dialect; her secretaries translated her words into Latin, not always with Arnaud's precision. Others again collected her thoughts and sayings second-hand, probably without even checking with her. These reports are generally accurate, but do not have the reliability of the original dictations. The last item reads in translation:

> The venerable Bride of Christ, Angela of Foligno, saved from the shipwreck of this world, passed into the heavenly joys promised to her long ago, in the year of the Incarnation 1309, on the vigil of the Nones of January, in the time of the Lord Pope Clement V.

Angela happened to live in troubled times for the Church.

Rome had revolted against the popes, who had been forced to flee to Perugia, then to Avignon in France. Deep-seated conflicts were raging between rigorist and laxist factions among the newly established Orders of Friars — the rigorists supporting a doctrine of extreme asceticism, while the laxists were teaching that the ideals of the Rule of St. Francis were impossible to attain. Friar Ubertin of Casale, who at the time fell into the error of excessive rigorism, gives this testimony concerning the difficulties encountered by Angela, and her beneficial influence:

> And so, in spite of the deeds of jealous people who denied the holiness of the blameless life of this very saintly soul, and the divine conversions wrought in the lives of many by her words and her merit, this Angela has been established by God for the sake of a crowd of spiritual sons as a mother of gracious love, of fear, of spiritual greatness and of holy hope. For every kind of good has come to them through her . . . . even to those who before had been excessively lax.

Angela, who was a member of the Third Order of St. Francis, displays an essentially Franciscan spirituality. As a powerful enemy of any libertarian excess, so widespread in the religious life of her time, she chose heroism, holiness, absolute poverty, frightful austerities, a high level of prayer, total love of God. While generally siding with the rigorists, she managed to stay clear of the bitter wranglings that surrounded her and caused her much suffering.

At no time did the Church authorities ever doubt her holiness. Immediately after her death on January 4, 1309, she was seen as a Blessed, and her feast received its proper office in 1701. The greatest theologians endorsed her works, among them St. Francis de Sales, Bossuet, Fenelon, Alphonsus of Liguori. Pope Benedict XIV venerated her as an equal of Teresa of Avila and John of the Cross. She deservedly received her place among the major women-mystics of all times.

The first nineteen steps of Angela's spiritual evolution, as

recorded by Brother Arnaud, correspond with the classical stages
of the mystical life: purification, illumination and union. Some of
the steps are described in a few lines, while others are elaborated.
In summary, the first sixteen steps are as follows:

1. The awareness of sin
2. Confession
3. Penance
4. Acknowledgment of God's mercy
5. Self-knowledge
6. Enlightening of grace
7. Turning the eyes toward the cross
8. Understanding Christ's death for our sins
9. Discovering the way of the cross
10. Asking God what would please him
11. Discovering the need for harsh penance
12. Giving up all property
13. Asking for a sign of approval
14. Vision of Christ's wounds
15. Suffering Christ's passion with Mary and John
16. Obtaining an understanding of the Lord's Prayer

We will now quote in full steps seventeen, eighteen and nineteen, in the words of Brother Arnaud, which indicate how Angela
increased in faith, hope and love.

THE BOOK OF THE EXPERIENCE OF THE
TRUE FAITHFUL (Excerpts)
*(The numbers correspond with those of the Droz edition, Paris,
1927)*

Note what follows concerning faith:

20.   In the *seventeenth* place, it was shown to me after this that
the blessed Virgin had acquired for me and given to me the grace of

a faith different from the one I had before — for it seemed to me that up to this point my faith had been like dead by comparison, and that my tears had been forced. But from then on, I suffered over the passion of Christ more genuinely and with the sorrow of the Mother of Christ. At that time, whatever I was doing and as much as I could do seemed little to me, and I wanted to perform a greater penance. And then I enclosed myself within Christ's passion. And the hope was given to me that there I could find my deliverance.

Note what follows concerning hope:

And then I began to receive consolations in my sleep, and I had many beautiful dreams, and I found great comfort in them. And I began to receive God's sweetness in my soul continuously, while awake or asleep. Yet, since until this point I had no feeling of certainty, sweetness was still mixed with bitterness: I wanted something more from God.

She told me one of her dreams or visions in these words:

Some time ago, I was in the cell *(literally,* the prison) where I had locked myself during Great Lent. I enjoyed and meditated over a saying of the Gospel that showed extreme condescension and love. I had a book next to me, a missal, and I wanted dearly to see that saying in writing. Afraid of acting out of pride, I held back, lest my hands open this book out of excessive desire and love. And still in the throes of this desire, I fell asleep. Immediately I was subject to a vision, and it was said to me that the understanding of the epistle *(sic)* was something so delightful, that if one could only grasp it properly, he would forget everything else in the world. And my guide asked me, "Do you want to try?" And as I agreed, he led me to this understanding. And I perceived the divine goods with such sweetness that I immediately forgot all the advantages of the world. And my guide told me that understanding the Gospel was so delightful that if only one could grasp it, he would forget not only all the advantages of the world, but even himself, completely. And he led me further and let me experience this as a fact. And immediately, I grasped the divine goods with such great pleasure that I forgot not only all the advantages of the world, but even myself. And I was in such a state of divine delight that I begged my guide never to let me lose it. And he told me that what I was asking could not as yet be granted. Then he brought me back, and I opened my eyes. I felt immense joy for what I had seen — but also immense sorrow for having lost it. And it still gives me great pleasure to recall it. And from this experience, there remained in me such certainty, such light, such burning love of God that I assure you most definitely that the pleasure of God is never preached properly in any sermon. And those who preach cannot preach it, and they cannot understand what they are talking about. My guide who led me during the vision told me so.

Note that in the preceding step, three things — faith, hope and love — are given to her perfectly.

21.   In the *eighteenth* place: After that, I had such a vivid feeling of God and perceived such great pleasure in prayer that I forgot to eat. And I wished I had no need of food so that I could remain in prayer. Thus did temptation creep in, that is, not to eat, or if I did, to eat very little — but I recognized it as a temptation. And such was the fire of the love of God in my heart that I never got tired of genuflections or other penitential practices. And this fire of the love of God in my heart became so intense that as soon as I heard someone speak of God, I cried out. And even if someone had wielded an ax over me to kill me, I could not have stopped my cries. And this happened to me for the first time when I sold my country estate to give to the poor. It was my best piece of land. First I had been making fun of Petruccio,* but now I could only do as he

---

*A holy man God had put on her way to lead her to total dispossession of her material goods. She had made fun of him at first, but now begins to imitate him generously.

had done. Even more: when people told me I was possessed by the devil because I had been forced to do what I had done — and this shamed me greatly — I would agree that indeed I might have been sick and possessed, and I could not answer those who were speaking ill of me. And whenever I caught sight of some picture of Christ's passion, I could hardly bear it: a fever would seize me, and I would become ill. And so my companion* did her best to hide from me any picture of the passion.

22.   In the *nineteenth* place: . . . After the revelation I had received in a marvelous fashion concerning the Our Father, I obtained a first major consolation from God's sweetness in this way: On one occasion, I was inspired and impelled to consider the pleasure there is in the contemplation of Christ's divinity and humanity. This was the greatest of the consolations I had perceived so far: it was so great that for most of the day I remained standing in the cell where I was praying, highly tensed and alone, but with a jubilant heart. Then I fell to the ground and lost the power of speech. When my companion came to me, she believed that I was going to die, that I was already in the grip of death. But I was annoyed, because she was interfering with this very great consolation.

At some other time, before she had completely given up all her goods, although she had very few left, the faithful of Christ was praying. It was in the evening, and she said it seemed she felt nothing of God, and she was praying and lamenting in these words:

Lord, whatever I am doing, I do only in order to find you! Let me find you when I have finished doing it!

And she said many other things in this prayer. And an answer came to her: What do you want? *She replied,* I want neither gold nor silver, and even if you offered me the whole universe, I would want nothing but you. *And he answered:* Hurry, for as soon as you

---

*A young girl identified only as Maria (M. in manuscripts) who lived with Angela at the time.

have completed what you are doing, the whole Trinity will enter you.

And at that time, he [God] promised me much more, and he relieved me of every tribulation, and he dismissed me very sweetly. From then on, I was expecting that what he had said would happen. I told my companion about it, still doubting because of the greatness of what had been revealed and promised to me. But God had dismissed me with great divine sweetness.

(In the following paragraphs, Arnaud describes Angela's visions in Assisi and her communications with the Trinity. Since this is extremely long and has been summarized earlier, we will now pick up her story as she returns home.)

36. After returning home, I felt within myself a tranquil sweetness so deep I cannot describe it. And I wanted to die. Living was for me such a pain because of this tranquil and quiet sweetness, this sweetness so deep I cannot describe it, but I desired to die to this world in order to go to this sweetness and not lose it. Living was for me a greater pain than the death of my mother and sons, and beyond any pain I could imagine. I lay at home in this supreme consolation and languor for eight days. And my soul cried out: "Lord, have mercy on me, and do not allow me to stay longer in this world." On the way to Assisi, he had foretold to me this unutterable sweetness and consolation, saying: "As soon as you have returned home, you will feel a sweetness different from anything you have ever perceived. Then I will not speak to you as I do now, but you will feel me." And I began to feel this unutterable or ineffable consolation, so tranquil and quiet I cannot express it, and I stayed in bed for eight days, and during that time I could hardly speak or say the Our Father. On the way to Assisi, he had said to me: "Many times I was with the apostles, and they saw me with bodily eyes, yet, they did not feel what you feel. As for you, you do not see me, but you do feel me."

When I realized all this was going to end, he retired most gently, and he said: "My daughter, you are sweeter to me than I am

to you." And he repeated what he had already said: "My temple!
My delight!" He did not want me to lie down while he was leaving,
so at these words I stood up. And he said to me: "You are holding
the ring of my love. I hold you close. From now on, you will never
leave me. You and your companion, may you have the blessings of
the Father and the Son and the Holy Spirit." He said that at the
moment of leaving, because I had sought a favor for my companion. And he answered me: "I give another favor to your
companion."

When he said, "From now on, you will never leave me," my
soul cried out: "Oh, I will never again commit a mortal sin!" But
he replied: "I am not saying that." Later, I often perceived
extraordinary fragrances. These experiences and others were so
tremendous I cannot explain them in words. I can repeat a little of
the words, but I cannot reproduce the sweetness and the pleasure.
Many more times were such things as these said to me, but never at
such length or so deeply and sweetly.

37. *How it was revealed to her companion that the Holy
Spirit dwelled in the faithful of Christ*

While she was lying in bed after returning from Assisi — as it
was said above — her companion heard a voice saying: "The Holy
Spirit is within L."*Immediately, she went to her and began to ask
her questions: "Tell me what you have, for these words were said
to me now." And the faithful of Christ answered her: "If you were
told, I will tell you." And she confirmed what had happened. From
then on, the faithful of Christ made known to her companion
several of the divine secrets.

38. *How the said companion saw over the faithful of Christ
something that looked like a many-colored star*

Later, this same companion told me, brother scribe, that on one
occasion when the faithful of Christ was lying on her side in a state

---

*L. stands for Lella, a diminutive of Angela. Seldom does Arnaud refer to her in any other
way than "the faithful of Christ."

of mental ecstasy, she saw something like a splendid star, of many resplendent colors. Rays of astonishing beauty shot out of the faithful of Christ, some thick, others thin. After surging from her breast as she lay on her side, they curved back as they rose to the sky. She saw this with her bodily eyes while she was wide awake. It was about three in the afternoon. The star was not very large.

39. *How a marvelous answer was given to the faithful of Christ concerning the Trinity*

One day, I, unworthy brother who have written down these divine words, was asking her how it was possible that it had been said to her in the preceding revelation, ''I am the Holy Spirit,'' and a little later, ''I am the one who was crucified for you.'' After I had asked her this, she went back home. Later, she met me again and answered in these terms: ''As I was going back home, I began to ponder, for I was having some doubts about what you had asked me — for when something doubtful is said to me, I too am seized with doubts, because I see myself as completely unworthy. And while I was doubting, this answer came to me: 'Ask him, Brother A., why it was said to him, ''The Trinity has already entered you.'' Tell him, ''It has already come, it has already come in you.'' Ask him how it could have come'.'' And it was given to me to understand that, although the Trinity had entered me, yet it was still in heaven and had not left heaven. And so, I did not yet understand, since it seemed to me he had not answered intelligibly or completely. The voice said: 'Tell him, ''When these words were said, 'I am the Holy Spirit,' and later, 'It is I who was crucified for you,' then Father, Son and Holy Spirit were within you.'' And since I doubted that the Father with the Son and the Holy Spirit had entered me, unworthy as I am, and since I was wondering whether this could not have been said to me for the sake of deception, it was repeated to me several times: 'It is indeed the Trinity that has entered you.' And then it was said to me: 'Ask him how I could have come.' And it was said to me that in this conversation Father, Son and Holy Spirit were present. And it seemed to me that I was being told that the Trinity was a single thing, made altogether one, but absolutely simple. And the example of the sun was given to me, together with other examples, but I rejected this, for when such great things are being said to me, I reject them out of fear of being unworthy. I wanted God to make me actually feel that on this point I could not be deceived.''

This point, "The whole Trinity will enter you," is noted in the preceding step, that is, towards the end of the eighteenth, and it was fulfilled in the twentieth.

40. *How Christ himself appeared to the faithful of Christ while she was meditating on his passion*

She said to me:"'One day I was meditating on the dreadful pains Christ endured on the cross. I was considering the nails which, as I had heard it said, had pressed the flesh of his hands and feet into the wood. And I wanted to see at least that small amount of Christ's flesh that had been pressed into the wood. This torture of Christ gave me such great sorrow that I could no longer stand on my feet. I bent over and sat down. I stretched out my arms on the ground and inclined my head on them. Then Christ showed me his breast and arms. Then my sorrow changed into a joy so intense I can say nothing of it. It was a joy different from any other. I could see, hear, feel nothing but it. There was so much light within my soul that I have no more doubt and will ask no further question. And he left this sign of joy with so much certainty in my soul that I believe I will never lose it. His breast and his neck were so beautiful I realized such beauty was divine. Hence, because of that beauty, it seemed to me I was seeing his divinity, and that I was standing in the presence of God — but nothing else was shown to me besides this. I cannot compare this illumination with any object or color of the world, except perhaps with the light of Christ's body, which I sometimes see at the elevation. And as I was coming out of this vision and began to regain consciousness, I had some slight doubts and afterthoughts. But when they came to me, I am quite certain I had already come out of this vision.''

41. *How she saw Christ in the Sacrament of the Altar*

I, brother scribe, when I heard what it seemed God had wanted her to say concerning the body of Christ, I noted it immediately in my heart. Then I asked her, I compelled her, to tell me everything she had ever seen in the body of Christ. Under my coercion, she began to talk: "Sometimes I see the host as I saw the neck and breast, with a splendor and beauty that seem to come from within and that exceed the splendor of the sun. Through this beauty, I am made to understand without doubt that I am seeing God. At home, however, I saw in this neck and breast a so much greater beauty that I believe I will never lose the joy of it. And I have no way to compare it except with the host containing the body of Christ, for in the host there appears a beauty superior to that of the sun, and much more so. But my soul is in great sorrow for being unable to express it."

She told me also that sometimes the host appears to her in a different way. She sees in it two magnificent eyes, so large it seems only the edges of the host are left. "But at other times, the eyes appeared to me, not in the host, but in my cell. Their beauty was so delightful that I believe I will never lose the joy of it — as with the breast. Yet, I don't know whether I was asleep or awake, but I found myself again in this immense and unutterable joy which I believe I will never lose."

On another occasion, she told me she had seen in the host a likeness of the Child Jesus — but he seemed great and sorrowful as one who holds dominion, and he was seen holding in his hand something like the symbol of power, and he was enthroned. "But I cannot say what he was holding in his hand. And this I saw with my bodily eyes, as everything I ever saw of the host. At that point, I did not kneel down like the others, and I don't know whether I ran up to the altar, or whether I was unable to move on account of this joy and vision. I was very much upset because the priest put down the host on the altar too soon. Jesus was so splendid, so majestic! He looked like a child of twelve. And it gave me such joy I believe I will never lose it. And the certainty of it was such that I doubt no single detail of it. Hence, it is not necessary for you to write it down. I was so delighted I did not even ask him to help me, nor did I say anything, good or bad, but enjoyed this beauty beyond measure.''

End of the first step concerning intimacy

(The recording of what follows runs to hundreds of pages, all of which are worth reading in the book *"The Experience of the True Faithful."* In the present study, however, we are offering only the highlights of Angela's extraordinary career.)

42. . . .On the road to Assisi, the Lord had said to her: ''I will perform in you great deeds before the nations; in you I shall be known, and my name shall be praised in you by many people.''

44. . . .''I am giving you a sign much better than the one you ask: this sign shall be at all times in your soul. You shall always feel something of God, and shall always be burning with love for him. And you will recognize in your inner being that no one but I can do such a thing. Here, then, is the sign I will imprint in the depth of your soul, a sign that is better than what you asked: I leave you a love so great your soul will be continually burning for me. So great shall be your love that if you are insulted, you will see the insult as a grace and will proclaim yourself unworthy of such a favor. For I myself have suffered all that, and so great was my love for you, I endured it patiently. At this sign, you will know I am with you.''

50. . . .''Work at loving with all your might, for you are much loved, and you will be transformed into something infinite.''

54. . . .''All those God teaches and enlightens in order that they may find his way, and who close their souls to this light and to this special teaching from God and harden their hearts; all those who know this teaching comes from God and follow a different one; all those who choose to follow the common way in spite of their conscience: all of them bear the curse of Almighty God.''

61.   On one occasion, she heard these divine words: "I who speak to you am the divine Might who bring you a favor. This is the favor I am bringing you: I want you to be useful to all who will see you. Even more: I want you also to help and be useful to all who think of you and who hear your name. The more someone will possess me, the more useful shall you be to him." Then, although my soul perceived a supreme joy, it replied: "I do not want this grace, I am afraid it may harm me, produce in me vainglory." He answered me immediately: "You can do nothing about it: this good is not yours, you are only its guardian. Keep it well, and give it back to its Owner." Then my soul understood this grace could do me no harm. Anyway, it had been said to me: "It pleases me that you have such fears."

64. . . . "It is when you feel yourself most abandoned that you are most loved by God, that God stands closest to you."

90. . . . "The more one feels God, the less one is able to say anything about him, for by the very fact of feeling something of this infinite and unutterable good, one becomes less capable of speaking of it."

105.   Thus spoke the faithful of Christ: "On a certain occasion, my soul was lifted up: I saw God in a light and fullness I had never seen him in before. But I saw no love. It is then I lost the love I had in me — I was made non-love!

"After that, I saw him in darkness, and precisely in darkness, because he is too great to be imagined or understood, and anything that can be thought or comprehended does not attain him, or even come close to him. Then my soul was given a very assured faith, a trusting and firm hope, a continuous certainty concerning God that removed all fear. And in this good that may be seen in darkness, I recollected myself entirely. I became so safe concerning God that I can never again doubt him, or doubt that I possess him in reality. And in this most effective good that is seen in darkness, my most assured hope is now fully recollected and safe."

(The experience recounted here by Angela corresponds with

the classical mystical state of the "dark night of the spirit," in which the soul is deprived of any awareness of God and is left in total darkness which faith alone can penetrate. On this faith, then, hope is rebuilt blindly. After hope, the love that had been based on rational evidence, and had therefore disappeared with the loss of the intellection of God, returns in a much higher form. This phenomenon is the door to the highest mystical state, that of union with God.)

121. . . . "I am lifted up and led by God to this state: I do not go to it on my own. I could not, and would not, nor do I desire it or ask for it. I now live in it continuously. Very often God lifts up my soul without asking for my consent. At certain times, when I am expecting it or thinking of it the least, suddenly my soul is lifted up by God. I dominate and embrace the whole world. It seems to me I am no longer on earth, but in heaven. Such is my actual state. It is much more excellent than any I have gone through so far: it entails so much fullness, light, certainty, nobility and expansion that I have the feeling no past condition comes anywhere near it." And the faithful of Christ told me she had enjoyed this unutterable manifestation of God more than a hundred thousand times, more than a million times, yet it was always new: each time, her soul had received something fresh, and whatever she had, she possessed in a novel and different way.

125. . . . "God himself also said to me: 'Everything that has been written has been written according to my will and has come from me, that is, it has proceeded from me.' Then he said, 'I will seal it.' And as I did not understand what he meant by 'I will seal it,' he continued, 'I will sign it.' ''

(Here ends the first part of Angela's story, the relation of the twenty-six steps. The second and third parts contain miscellaneous documents collected by Arnaud and others. All are worth reading, but would add an excessive burden to the present study.) Perhaps the best way to conclude would be to quote the closing paragraph of her final work, the *Little Treatise on Love:*

207.   ''Those who are lifted up to the vision of the Uncreated and of the being of God by standing before the cross and practicing the works of virtue, are at rest wherever they happen to be. Their love renews itself and rekindles itself in order to act with greater efficiency. But those who are not living in truth fashion idols out of their works and virtues. And the first idol is the one they make out of the divine light that was given to them.''

IV

DAME JULIAN OF NORWICH

DAME JULIAN OF NORWICH
(1342- ?)

In many ways, Julian of Norwich is a mystery. No one seems to know her family name, nor her place of origin, nor is even her baptismal name certain: Some call her Juliana, others Julian, while the chronicler of Marjorie Kemp — another woman mystic of the same period — calls her Dame Jelyan. Perhaps the name under which she is known has nothing to do with her baptismal name. It may simply be a corruption of the descriptive epithet, "the Dame of St. Julian" applied to her because she lived in a cell or group of cells attached to the cathedral church of St. Julian of Norwich. This hypothesis seems to explain the mystery of her being known under the male patronym of Julian. The little that is revealed of her personal life results from an analysis of her writings — but she speaks very little of herself, only as much as is necessary to give authenticity to her message.

The time of Julian's birth has been established as late 1342, because in reporting the revelation she received on May 8, 1373, she says she was "thirty and one half years old."

Julian was not a member of a religious community, but an "anchoress," that is, a woman living alone in a state of poverty and chastity similar to that of a religious, and devoting her life to prayer and meditation, as would a contemplative nun. She managed to maintain her anonymity until the end: the date and manner of her death are unknown.

This complete lack of personal information was deliberate: Julian sought all along to focus people's attention upon her message and upon God, while hiding herself as much as possible as the humble instrument of the supernatural. She actually says so clearly:

"And therefore I beg you all for God's sake, and counsel you for your own good: Stop looking at the wretch to whom this revelation was shown. Intently, wisely and humbly look at God, who because of his courteous love and enduring goodness wills to show it to every one of us for our comfort."

Julian's first "Revelation" began on May 8, 1342, in the presence of two witnesses, her mother and the local curate. They could not see or hear anything of what was being revealed, but they fully realized that something mysterious and important was going on. There were other witnesses, but these two seem to have been present through the full course of the sixteen revelations, which lasted until the following day.

"Of these fifteen revelations, the first began early in the morning, about four o'clock, and they lasted — shown in a beautiful manner and in logical order — until past noon that day." (Chapter 65).

The sixteenth revelation was received the following day.

She explains how these revelations were conveyed to her:

"The whole revelation was shown in three ways: through my bodily eyes, through words formed in my intellect, and through spiritual insight. But the spiritual insight, I am neither allowed nor able to show as clearly and fully as I would like. Yet, I trust in our Lord God Almighty that, through his goodness and out of love for you, he may give you an understanding of it more sweetly and spiritually than I ever could or may." (Chapter 9).

As is the case with all mystics, Julian is at a loss to express the depth and splendor of the spiritual revelations she received. Her attitude towards them shows both her common-sense and her humility.

"I am not good because of the revelations, but only if I love God the better for it. And in the measure in which you love God better than I do, it is more profitable to you than to me. I am saying this, not to the wise, for they already know it well, but to you who are simple, for your ease and comfort, since we are all one in love. Indeed, it was not shown to me that he loved me any more than he loves the least soul in the state of grace. And I am sure there are many who have never had a revelation or a vision, but only the common teaching of Holy Church, who love God better than I do.'' (Chapter 9).

''It is known that before miracles come sorrow, anguish and trouble. This is intended to make us realize our own weakness and the wretchedness we have incurred through sin. It humbles us and makes us fear God and cry out for help and grace.'' (Chapter 36).

Julian accepts both favors and tribulations as gifts of love:

''This vision was shown to my intellect to teach me that it is good for some souls to have such an experience — alternations of comfort with distress and abandonment. God wants us to know that he is safeguarding us, as much in woe as in happiness. For the good of his soul, a man is sometimes left to himself, without sin being the cause of it — since at the time I had committed no sin that would have caused me to be left to myself: it happened unexpectedly. Nor did I deserve to enjoy the feeling of blessedness: our Lord gave it to me freely, as he pleased. And sometimes he allows us to suffer misery — but both are one and the same love.'' (Chapter 15).

In the same spirit, Julian quotes from memory the words Jesus addressed to her:

''Do not blame yourself as if you were responsible for your tribulations or miseries: I do not want you to be imprudently depressed and sad — for I tell you, whatever you do, you will have sorrow. That is why I want you to be wisely aware of the state of penance in which you always dwell, and to accept it as your personal penance. And then you shall truly see that all this living of yours is profitable penance.'' (Chapter 77).

Such counsel should be heard and pondered by all who suffer,

that is, by every one of us. Julian, in another chapter, again quotes
Jesus' words to her:

"Pray inwardly, even if you feel no reward: it is profitable
enough even if you feel nothing, see nothing, yes, even if it seems
you can do nothing. In dryness and barrenness, in sickness and
weakness, your prayer is most pleasing to me (though you seem to
have little taste for it). And so it is in my sight with all your prayers
of faith." (Chapter 41).

Such counsels, again, are of universal value, since barrenness
and a feeling of uselessness seem to be the bane of all who pray.

What do the sixteen revelations contain? They do not seem to
follow any logical order, but are all related to a vivid experience of
Christ, in his teaching, his agony and his death:

    1 — The Crowning of Thorns
    2 — The Discoloration of Jesus' Face
    3 — God Brings About Everything That Is Done
    4 — The Scourging and the Shedding of Blood
    5 — Overcoming the Devil
    6 — The Heavenly Reward of God's Servants
    7 — Both Happiness and Woe are Blessings
    8 — The Final Suffering and the Death of Christ
    9 — The Trinity's Pleasure Caused by Salvation
    10 — The Breaking of the Blessed Heart Because of Love
    11 — The Spiritual Manifestation of Jesus' Mother
    12 — God is the All-Sovereign Being
    13 — God Intends That We Revere His Deeds
    14 — God Is the Ground of Our Prayer
    15 — All Pain Will Be Alleviated
    16 — The Eternal Indwelling of the Trinity in the Soul.

Explanations of these sixteen revelations are interspersed with
chapters containing insights on them gained during Julian's twenty

years of prayer-life. This constitutes chapters 1 to 66. Another nineteen chapters offer further commentaries.

We are quoting the most interesting themes of her work under the following headings:

1 — Creation Is Small Compared With God's Immensity
2 — The Splendor of the Human Soul
3 — The Need for Trials and Humility
4 — All Manner of Things Shall Be Well
5 — The Only Necessary Thing
6 — God Is Our Mother
7 — The Final Message of Love

All quotations of Julian are offered in our own interpretation of the original.

1 — CREATION IS SMALL COMPARED WITH GOD'S IMMENSITY

"He [God] also showed me a little object, the size of a hazelnut, that seemed to lie in the palm of his hand: it was as round as a ball. I looked at it with the eyes of my intellect and wondered, 'What can this be?' And I was answered in general terms in this way: 'It is all that is made.' I was astonished at this, for it was so small it seemed it could vanish at any moment. And I answered in my mind: 'It lasts, and shall forever last, because God loves it. This is how everything has being: by God's grace.'" (Chapter 5).

"I know well that heaven and earth and all that is made is great and vast and beautiful and good. The reason why it appeared so small to me is that I was looking at it in the presence of its Maker. For to a soul that sees the Maker of all things, all that is made seems very little." (Chapter 8).

Everything created by God was made because God loved it. Now, since God's love endures forever, everything created will endure forever under one aspect or another. This calls for the redemption and eternal bliss, not only of mankind, but also of the lesser species, even of the vegetable and mineral worlds. How this will come about is very much God's secret, but Christ became incarnate to save not only man, but the whole universe.

2 — THE SPLENDOR OF THE HUMAN SOUL

"For as the body is clothed in garments, and the flesh in the skin, and the bones in the flesh, and the heart in the breast, so are we, soul and body, clothed and enclosed in God's goodness. Yes, and even more closely, for all these may waste and disappear, but God's goodness is ever whole and much closer to us than anything else." (Chapter 6).

"I understood that man's soul is made from nothing. That is to say, it is made, but not out of anything pre-existing — as when God fashioned man's body, he took the slime of the earth, which is mixed matter, a blend of all bodily things, and he made man's body out of it. For the making of man's soul, he took nothing at all: he simply made it. And so is created human nature rightfully one with its Maker, who is substantially uncreated nature — that is, God. And that is why there can and shall never be anything whatsoever between God and man's soul." (Chapter 53).

"I saw the soul as large as if it were an endless universe, and also as if it were a blessed, happy kingdom. And by the institutions I saw in it, I realized the soul is a glorious city. In the center of that city is enthroned our Lord Jesus, true God and true man, handsome, tall, the greatest Bishop, the most inspiring King, the Lord of highest glory. . . .

"For as well as the Father could make a creature, and as well as the Son could make a creature, so well did the Holy Spirit will that man's soul be made — and so it was made. Therefore the blessed Trinity rejoices without end in the making of man's soul, for he saw without beginning what would please him without end." (Chapter 67).

One of the themes of Gnostic theology — that there are many

intermediate spirits between God and the soul — is here formally denied, in favor of a theory of direct, existential contact, at the same time more awesome and more reassuring. This corresponds precisely with the official position of the Church, as do all of Julian's propositions. What she has done mainly is to take well-known dogmatic statements, and shed on them a new, refreshing and invigorating light issuing from her feminine intuition.

Julian may have been unable to read or write, but her mental faculties were highly developed, enriched as they were by her life of prayer and meditation, as revealed in the notes taken down by her scribe more than twenty years after the events.

3 — THE NEED FOR TRIALS AND HUMILITY

"I saw that the Lord rejoices in his servants' tribulations, but with pity and compassion. Upon every person he loves, in order to bring them to his bliss, he imposes something that is not a defect in his sight, but is a reason why they are humbled and despised in this world, scorned, mocked and cast out. This he does to prevent the harm they would suffer from the pretense and vanities of this wretched life, to make ready their way to heaven and to the state of eternal happiness. For he says, 'I shall tear you away from your vain affections and vicious pride. Then I shall gather you, and make you meek and mild, pure and holy by uniting you to me.' " (Chapter 28).

"By contrition, we are made clean; by compassion, we are made ready; and by true longing for God, we are made worthy. These are the three means, as I saw it, by which all souls — that is, all former sinners on earth — will come to heaven and shall be saved. By these medicines are all sinful souls to be healed. And after they are healed, their wounds are seen before God, not as wounds, but as marks of honor, . . . for he sees sin as sorrow and pain to his lovers, to whom, out of love, he assigns no blame. The reward we shall receive shall be not little, but high, glorious and exalting. And so, even shame shall be transformed into honor and joy. Our gentle Lord does not want his servants to despair because of the number or gravity of their sins, for our failures are no obstacle to his love.'' (Chapter 39).

Julian reminds us of our frailty, of our habitual sinning, and of the road to repentance and redemption. She uses a paradox in making the scars of repented sins appear as marks of glory.

A similar thought is expressed by Christ when he says there will be more rejoicing in heaven for a single sinner who repents than for ninety-nine just who have no need of repentance. There is obvious irony here in the word ''Just'': Christ is not disparaging or discouraging the truly just; he is referring to people who are so self-righteous they manage to persuade themselves they have no need of repentance. In the parable of the Prodigal Son, the attitude of the elder brother is an example of such self-righteousness, and the welcome given to the prodigal, an example of rejoicing in heaven.

But Julian does seem to say that the suffering endured as a consequence of sin may procure merit. This is an extreme extension of the notion of *felix culpa* — the fertile, fruitful sin of Adam without which Christ might not have become incarnate. For centuries, a controversy raged in the Church on this particular point: *si non pecasset,* if Adam had not sinned, would Christ have become incarnate? The question makes no sense, for in fact the Bible tells us that Adam did sin — and he is still sinning in man's propensity toward evil we call concupiscence. No sin as such can ever be the cause or condition of a morally good effect. Julian herself cautions against any misinterpretation of her thought.

''But now, if any man or woman, because of this spiritual consolation I have described, would be foolishly tempted to say or think, 'If this be true, it may be good to sin in order to obtain a greater reward,' or to see less evil in sin, let him beware of such temptation. Indeed, if the thought comes, it is false and from the enemy. For this same true Love who teaches us by his blessed comfort, also teaches us to hate sin alone, out of love." (Chapter 40).

The scar of repented sin is a mark of glory *relative to the evil of sin,* and not in any absolute sense, so that it would be foolish indeed to sin in order to obtain the glory of repentance. Here again the truly just are vindicated.

"We must needs fall, and we must needs see it. If we did not fall, we would never find out on our own how weak and wretched we are, nor would we know so fully our Maker's marvelous love...

"A mother may allow her child to fall occasionally, and suffer different kinds of discomforts for its own good. But because of her love, this excludes exposure to any real danger." (Chapter 61.)

There is here an indication of a solution to the problem of evil: without the possibility of falling — and its actuality — there would be no merit, no effort, no deserved reward. Good is possible only in opposition to evil. The point made here by Julian seems to be that somehow or other, even sin will be straightened out at the end.

4 — ALL MANNER OF THINGS SHALL BE WELL

This, perhaps, is the core of Julian's teaching, that for which she is best remembered. The expression, "All manner of things shall be well," has become almost a proverb. It is quoted and expanded, among other places, in T.S. Eliot's *"Four Quartets. 1"* *Here we will let Julian speak for herself.*

"Sin has to happen, but all shall be well. All shall be well, and all manner of things shall be well.

"Through this naked word, 'sin,' the Lord brought to my mind everything in general that is not good: the shameful contempt and utter annihilation he suffered for us in this life; his dying and all the spiritual and bodily pains of his creatures. For all of us are, at least in part, reduced to nothing, and shall so be reduced, following our Master Jesus, until we are fully cleansed, that is, until we are fully stripped of our mortal flesh and of all those inner affections of ours that are not really good. . . .

"Because of the tender love our Lord has for all those who are to be saved, he comforts them swiftly and sweetly, saying 'It is true that sin is the cause of all this pain, but all shall be well. All shall be well, and all manner of things shall be well.'

"These words were said most tenderly, without implying any blame to me or to anyone else of the future elect. . . .

"In these same words, I saw a marvelous high secret hidden in God — to be made known to us openly in heaven. By knowing it, we shall truly see why he allowed sin to come, and in this sight, we shall rejoice forever in our Lord God." (Chapter 27).

"God's servants, Holy Church, shall be shaken with sorrow, anguish and tribulation in this world, as men shake a cloth in the wind. But to this, our Lord answered in these words: 'A great thing I shall make of this in heaven, a thing of endless exaltation and everlasting joy.' " (Chapter 28).

"He showed that Adam's sin was the greatest harm that was ever done, or that shall ever be done until the end of the world. And he also showed that this is clearly known on earth throughout the Holy Church. Furthermore, he taught me that I should consider the glorious remedy: for this making amends is incomparably more pleasing to God and more effective for man's salvation than ever Adam's sin was harmful." (Chapter 29).

"Thus did the good Lord answer all the questions and doubts I could come up with, saying most comfortingly, 'I may make all things well, I can make all things well, I intend to make all things well, and I shall make all things well. And you shall see for yourself that all manner of things shall be well.'

"When he says, 'I may,' I understand he means the Father; when he says, 'I can,' the Son; when he says, 'I intend,' the Holy Spirit; and when he says, 'I shall,' the unity of the Blessed Trinity — three Persons and one Truth. When he says, 'You shall see for yourself,' I understand the joining into one of all mankind that shall be saved in the blissful Trinity." (Chapter 31).

"At one time, our good Lord said, ' All things shall be well,' and at another, he said, 'You shall see for yourself that all manner of things shall be well.' Of these two sayings, the soul received different interpretations. One was that he wants us to understand that he pays attention, not only to noble and great matters, but also to little and small, lowly and simple things. He is concerned with both the one and the other. This is what he means when he says, 'All manner of things shall be well.' He wants us to understand that even the least of things shall not be forgotten.

"Another interpretation is this: As we can see, many evil deeds are being performed, and so great is the damage they inflict, it seems to us impossible that things should ever come out all right. As we consider these deeds, we sorrow and mourn, which prevents us from being at rest in the blissful contemplation of God, as we ought to be. And that is because our present method of reasoning is so blind, so low and so naive that we cannot conceive the lofty and marvelous wisdom, the power and the goodness of the Blessed Trinity. This is what he means when he says, 'You shall see for yourself that all manner of things shall be well,' as if he were saying, 'Accept it now, faithfully and trustfully, and at the last end, you shall see it in truth, in the fullness of joy. . . .'

"There is a deed the Blessed Trinity shall do on the last day, as I saw it, but what it shall be and how it shall be done is hidden to all creatures below Christ, until the time it shall come about. What our Lord God's goodness and love wants us to know is that the deed *shall* be done. Because of the same love, his power and wisdom choose to hide and conceal from us what it shall be and how it shall be done.

"The reason why he wants us to know this much, is that he wants us to be more at ease spiritually and more peaceful in love — and to stop looking at all the storms that could keep us from finding true joy in him. . . .

"Just as the Blessed Trinity made everything out of nothing, so

the same Blessed Trinity shall make well everything that is not
well.'' (Chapter 32).

''In the last word, he said, with true, full faithfulness, referring
to all of us: 'You shall not be overcome.' And all this teaching, and
this true comfort, are intended in general for all my fellow-
Christians, as I have said before. Such is God's will.

''The words, 'You shall not be overcome,' were said very
sharply and powerfully, as a safeguard and comfort against any
tribulation that may come. He did not say, 'You shall not be
troubled,' or, 'You shall not be burdened with hard labor,' or,
'You shall not be afflicted,' but, 'You shall not be overcome.' God
wants us to pay attention to these words, and that we be always
strong in faithful trust, whether in happiness or sorrow, for he loves
us and delights in us, and he wants us likewise to love him and
delight in him and have full confidence in him — and all shall be
well.'' (Chapter 68).

5 — THE ONLY NECESSARY THING

Julian appeals to God, and in the surprising way of the mystic,
receives clear and direct answers.

''O God, out of your goodness, give me yourself, for you are
enough for me. I can ask nothing less that would be fully to your
glory. And if I do ask anything less, I will always be in need, since
it is only in you that I have all!'' (Chapter 5).

''See, I am God! See, I am in all things! See, I do all things!
See, I never take my hands off my work, nor ever shall. See, I lead
all things to the end I ordained for them from eternity, by the same
power, wisdom and love with which I made them. How could
anything go wrong?'' (Chapter 11).

''Our Lord often said to me: 'I am It! I am the One! I am what is
highest! I am what you love! I am what delights you! I am what you
serve! I am what you long for! I am what you want! I am what you
intend! I am everything that is! I am what the Holy Church preaches

and teaches you! I am the One who showed myself to you here!' "
(Chapter 26).

Without using any of the classical and somewhat worn-out
expressions of the deity — the Alpha and the Omega, the Beginning and the End, the King of Kings, etc. — Julian expresses the
same notion of absolute dominance by repeating the words Jesus
spoke to her. Only Christ in person, the incarnate Son of God,
could have applied such attributes to himself. In the mouth of any
creature, such statements would be signs of megalomaniac insan-
ity. Coming from Christ, they make complete sense, confirming
the Gospel teaching, *"I am the Truth and the Way and the Life"*
(John 14:16).

6 — GOD OUR MOTHER

There are several references to God's motherhood in the works
of Julian of Norwich. The following few will suffice for our
purpose.

"God rejoices in that he is our Mother." (Chapter 52).

"The deep wisdom of the Trinity is our Mother, in whom we
are enclosed." (Chapter 54).

"God All-Wisdom is our Mother. . . .

"The Second Person of the Trinity is our Mother by nature, in
our substantial making. In it, we are grounded and rooted, and it is
our Mother by mercy in our bodies, by incarnation." (Chapter 59).

"Thus Jesus Christ, who does good as opposed to evil, is our
true Mother: we receive our being from him in whom the ground of
motherhood begins with all the sweet preservation of love that
follows without end. . . .'I am It, the Wisdom and Nature of
Motherhood.' " (Chapter 59).

Julian is not alone in teaching us about the feminine
characteristics of God. In a world dominated by males — from the
Jewish Old Testament, to the Moslem elimination of women from
heaven, to the present chauvinism — there have been many voices

attempting to re-establish a true balance by feminizing the
Godhead. St. Francis de Sales speaks of God as his "Motherly
Father." The same idea is found in the works of a contemporary
Chinese Catholic scholar, Doctor John C.H.Wu.

Of course, there is no sex in God, but since there are definite
sexual distinctions in the human race, our thoughts are influenced
by them to the point that we are unable to imagine a rational being
who is not either male or female. In the Western world, the general
tendency has been to identify God the Father with the male,
bearded Zeus of Greek mythology. Christ was definitely a man.
Some authors attribute feminine characteristics to the Holy Spirit.
All this, however, is anthropomorphism: the bad habit of attributing to beings of a different order the distinctions proper to
mankind.

By calling God and Jesus our Mother, Julian is merely com-
pensating for an excessively male theology — and in this, she is
quite right.

7 — THE FINAL MESSAGE OF LOVE

"And thus I understood that any man or woman who delib-
erately chooses God in this life, out of love, may be sure that he or
she is loved without end. This endless love produces grace in them.
For God wants us to hold trustfully to this: that we be as certain, in
hope, of the bliss of heaven while we are here as we will be, in fact,
when we are there. And always the more delight and joy we take in
this certainty, with reverence and meekness, the better it pleases
him." (Chapter 65).

"Some of us believe God is almighty and may do everything,
and that he is all-wise and can do everything — but that he is all
love and *shall* do all, that we fail to see." (Chapter 73).

"From the time of the revelation, I often wondered what our
Lord's meaning was, and more than fifteen years later, I was
answered by a spiritual understanding: 'Do you want to know your

Lord's meaning in this event? Know it well: love was his meaning. Who showed it to you? Love! What did he show you? Love! Why did he show it? For the sake of Love! Keep yourself therein: you shall know more about it, but you will never know differently in it, throughout eternity.' '' (Chapter 86).

How God is to achieve the final conciliation of all opposites, the final reward of all virtue and the punishment of all vice into one stupendous unity of love, is to remain beyond man's understanding until judgment day. But even though we may not understand *how* it is to come about, the promise that it *will* come about is a tremendous consolation for people of good will, particularly in such times of fear and darkness as the nuclear age we are living through.

In our limited human understanding, we all have great difficulty coping with the suffering of the innocent, the death of children, cruel and ravaging diseases. Too often we see vice triumphant while virtue remains unrewarded; we see people enjoying a wealth they have acquired dishonestly, or by crushing anyone who ever dared to stand in their way; we see many abuses of power in governments and even in the Church, and many wars waged in the name of God. If the present life were the only one, there would be good reason to despair. We are tempted to believe that if all such injustices are allowed, there is no just God and all religion is vain. The tendency, then, is to embrace cynicism, to join in the dog-eat-dog competition of the business world, and to ease our conscience with the belief that, since there is no justice, we are free to make the most of whatever we can get away with.

Such is the short view of our times, the human view of people whose perspective is limited to a segment of time and a minute area of the world. Even within this restricted span, it is sometimes possible to see God's justice at work: crime may be punished on the spot. A report was published in the twenties about the ten richest men of the times — all of whom died early or violently, by accident, suicide or assassination. In many other cases, however, criminals seem to be enjoying in peace the fruits of their misdeeds, while the children of light suffer neglect and poverty.

It is here that Julian's message acquires all its importance: it helps us see reality through the eyes of God, in its complete fullness, from beginning to end, when all injustice shall be straightened out and every good deed rewarded. Understanding how this will come about is beyond the scope of our imagination, but faith, supported by the mystics' prophetic visions, allows us to accept as a remote but certain fact the ultimate reality of love.

Love is much more than an emotional attachment: it is a creative, active and dynamic principle, the power that made the world to be and that sustains it in its present existence, and the final goal toward which it tends. It is the origin and purpose of the creation of our own selves, and our final destination. Love is not only what makes the world go round; it is what made creation come about in the first place, and it will keep it going on forever through God's mysterious final deed, so that, as Julian put it, "All manner of things shall be well." Alleluia!

V

JOSEFA MENÉNDEZ

JOSEFA MENÉNDEZ
(1890-1923)

A survey of female mystical experience would be incomplete without at least one example of the extremes of sacrifice and suffering of some of God's handmaids, in the tradition of John of the Cross and Thérèse of Lisieux. The passionate approach, characteristic of the Iberian temperament, appears clearly in the writings of Josefa Menéndez, a Spanish Sister of the Society of the Sacred Heart of Jesus, who lived all of her religious life in France.

Josefa Menéndez was born in Madrid on the 4th of February, 1890, the daughter of Leonardo Menéndez — an officer and artist, painter of military scenes — and Lucia del Moral, an excellent wife and mother. Three girls were born after Josefa, and two boys who died young.

Leonardo taught his eldest daughter himself, hoping she would become a teacher, but a very definite religious vocation developed at an early age.

On the third day of her First-Communion retreat, at age 11, she composed this written offering:

> On this day, 19th of March, 1901, before all heaven and earth, taking as my witness my heavenly mother Mary, and St. Joseph as my advocate and father, I promise Jesus that I will forever safeguard in me the precious virtue of virginity, my only desire being to please him, and my only fear, that of offending him by sin. Show me, O God, how to belong entirely to thee in the most perfect manner possible, that I may ever love thee more and more, and never displease thee

in anything. This is the desire of my heart on this, my
First-Communion day. Holy Mary, I beg you, on this feast-
day of your holy spouse St. Joseph, to obtain approval of my
petition. Your loving child,

Josefa Menéndez

When she told her spiritual director, Father R. F. Rubio, what
she had done, he explained to her that little girls should not make
promises beyond that of being very good, and he wanted her to tear
up the paper. But she could not, and continued to repeat, "Lord, I
am thine forever!"

Josefa was educated with her sisters in the Sacred Heart Free
School, where she began her close contact with the Blessed Sacrament through daily visits to the chapel. In 1907, death and suffering that were to become so much part of her life invaded the happy
household: within a few weeks, one of the little girls died of a
sudden illness, their grandmother followed soon after, and their
father and mother became sick — he of typhoid fever, she of
pneumonia. Josefa and her two remaining sisters were suddenly
destitute, reduced to sleeping on a mattress on the floor.

Fortunately, the nuns of the Sacred Heart were watching over
them. They gave Josefa some work and a sewing machine. With
her ability as a dressmaker, Josefa managed to keep her little family
going.

The father, Leonardo, died of a heart attack in 1910, and Josefa
remained the sole support of her mother and sisters. Even before
her father's death, she had expressed the desire to join the Society
of the Sacred Heart, but her parents had not allowed her to do so.
Later, her mother permitted one of her younger sisters to enter as a
novice at the Sacred Heart Convent of Chamartin in Madrid.
Josefa's disappointment needed all of her faith in God to be borne
in peace.

In 1912, Father Rubio, who was closely observing her vocation, suggested she enter the convent of the Order of Mary Reparatrix. She was eventually admitted, but immediately realized it was not her true home. After six months of postulantship had elapsed, her mother came to the convent in tears and claimed her. Josefa courageously returned to her dressmaking.

At the time, "Les Feuillants," the French motherhouse of the Society of the Sacred Heart founded by St. Madeleine Sophie Barat, was being reopened after its closure by iniquitous anti-religious laws. On the 16th of September, 1919, when Josefa was already twenty-nine, a letter arrived at Chamartin, from "Les Feuillants," asking for novices. The Superior offered Josefa the opportunity to go. This time, her mother was unable to resist any longer. At last, with her heart breaking at the thought of abandoning her family forever and entering a convent in a foreign land the language of which she did not understand, she left for her new assignment. She was never to see Spain again.

What followed was a life of trials, sufferings and ecstasies outlined in the following section.

Besides her family trials and the long and painful waiting for her vocation to be fulfilled, Josefa's sufferings began in earnest as soon as she arrived in Les Feuillants:

> *May 7, 1919* — "Yes, dear Lord, I will stay here; I love you and I will obey. I can see no light, but in spite of this, I will be faithful to you."

This is a characteristic phase of the mystical life — the "Dark Night of the Senses," which often serves as a prelude to illumination. On the 16th of July, 1920, Josefa's postulantship ended together with her trials and temptations. All of a sudden, she was, as she naïvely expresses it, "wrapped in a sweet slumber," from which she awoke in the wounds of the Sacred Heart. In the radiance now illuminating her, she saw all the sins of the world, and offered her life to comfort the wounded Heart. This seems to be the first instance of mystical ecstasy — an experience she was to go through many times in the course of the last three years of her life.

All the while, Josefa was being pursued by the devil whose voice was constantly telling her she was making straight for perdition — but the voices of Mary and Jesus reassured her:

> *October 15, 1920* — Mary said: "Do not be afraid of suffering, for you will always be given sufficient strength to bear it. Think of this: you have only today in which to suffer and love. Eternity will be all joy."
>
> *July 8, 1921* — Jesus said: "When you are in pain, I rest, and my heart rejoices in converse with you. Have no fear, for my visits will never harm you: you are in my hands, and I will guard you, provided you refuse me nothing."

The whole mystery of mystical suffering is contained in this quotation. Although Josefa is to die from this suffering, no true harm will come to her since this sharing in Christ's passion is a condition of eternal glory.

All the demon's efforts, during a long period of nine months, were concentrated on the destruction of Josefa's vocation. He spared nothing to bend her to his will: violent temptations, fear of a crushing responsibility, perfidious falsehoods, obsessions that endowed her with a dual personality and made her think what she did not believe and do what she did not want to do — without allowing her to discern that she was under diabolic domination. Deceptive and menacing appearances, blows, abductions and burnings, all were hurled at the frail child as a hurricane in which it would seem she must suffer shipwreck.

At times she was whisked away, twisted and tucked into impossible corners under the attic rafters, from which the Mother Superior or Assistant Superior had to go and release her. At other times, her clothing was burned on her very body. She was buffeted like St. John Vianney, bruised and thrown to the ground. That she did manage to resist was surely the result of divine strength.

A great power over her was being given to Satan, who opened before her the bottomless depths of hell itself. She was steeped in agonies never before experienced, and knew by sharp physical pain what the loss of a soul really meant, and how total was the immolation demanded of her for its redemption.

Josefa frequently endured this martyrdom. To those watching, only a slight tremor made known her mysterious state. Her body instantly became entirely limp and motionless, like one whose soul had just departed. Head and members were no longer under her control, though her heart beat normally. She was as one alive, yet dead. She let her whole soul pour out its tale of woe into the compassionate heart of her Lord:

> *April 16, 1922* — Jesus said: "Where is your faith? If I allowed you to be the devil's sport, know that I did it solely to give an unimpeachable proof of the plans of my heart for you."

Persecution by the devil was particularly severe before her first vows, which she took on July 16, 1922, a day of special grace, after which Jesus often came to her at night and gave her his cross to bear.

Then began a new phase in Josefa's life: she was to become the messenger of Jesus to the world. With great solemnity, he made her promise never to refuse what he asked of her. That night, when Josefa began to transcribe, as she usually did, the messages she had received during the day, she was so deeply struck by the Lord's solemn words that she dared not continue to write out of fear of relating them inaccurately. He reassured her, and instead of letting her write from memory, he dictated to her the important text of August 6, 1922 (see below).

In October, 1922, Josefa was entrusted with the making of school uniforms. She also helped when all were called to general work in the laundry, and she had care of three chapels, which she kept exquisitely clean. It is good to remember that besides her extraordinary mystical experience, she was incessantly active with humble work she performed so well that none of the sisters knew anything until her death about the spiritual and physical torments she was suffering almost daily.

On October 8, 1923, Josefa suffered a slight hemorrhage from the lungs. The doctor who examined her asked her age. She was thirty-three. He expressed his astonishment, saying, "She is worn out!" Persecutions weakened her even more. Through the promptings of the devil, she was now persuaded that the experiences of the last three years had been nothing but illusions. Since the beginning of November, Josefa's physical sufferings by day and principally by night had been destroying her, while intolerable pains, the cause of which could not be ascertained, increased in severity every Friday.

The last page of Josefa's diary is dated December 9, 1923. It seems that after that she was too weak to write.

The last few days of Josefa's life are again a succession of sufferings and consolations. In the morning of December 29, the Blessed Sacrament was brought to her for the last time. In the evening, at half-past seven, the sister infirmarian asked if she could do anything for her. Night had now fallen. "I am all right," she answered. "You can leave me alone." The Angelus was ringing and she knew it was time for the community supper.

Josefa — who had never been alone since December 9 — was now left by herself. And it was in this solitude, in this abandonment willed by God, that the Master came swiftly and fetched his privileged Little One, allowing her to die like himself: abandoned by all.

When a few minutes later the sister infirmarian returned, Josefa was dead. She was lying with her head slightly tilted back, her eyes half-closed and an expression of intense pain on her face. Almost at once, it changed to one of serenity and peace.

On November 13, 1923, shortly before her death, the Lord had said to Sister Josefa: "My words will be light and life for an incalculable number of souls, and I will grant them special graces of conversion and illumination.'' These words have been verified, for as soon as a small volume translated into French *(Un appel à l'amour, An Appeal to Love)* appeared in 1938, it was eagerly seized upon and reprinted several times, while letters from all parts of the world gave testimony to the profound impression created by it. Numerous translations were made. The first edition was endorsed by a letter in French by Cardinal Eugene Pacelli, later to become Pope Pius XII. It reads in translation:

Very Reverend Mother,

I have no doubt whatever that the publication of these pages will be agreeable to the Sacred Heart of Jesus, filled as they are with the great love which his grace inspired in his very humble servant Maria Josefa Menéndez.

May they efficiently contribute to the development in many souls of a confidence ever more loving and complete in the infinite mercy of this Divine Heart towards the poor sinners we all are.

These are the good wishes which, with my blessing, I send you and all the Society of the Sacred Heart.

E. Card. Pacelli

Only two months before her death, Josefa was called to Rome in fulfillment of a message from the Mother of God received on August 20, 1923. She went there from October 2 to October 26 of the last year of her life, 1923. The Mother General of the Society, who had wished for a long time to meet her, received her kindly. Most of her time was spent in writing down a message which has not been published and still remains the secret of the Society. St. Madeleine Sophie Barat appeared to her several times with messages of reassurance.

After her death, Josefa's writings were scrutinized by religious authorities. In 1926, after careful examination of the notes, a Consultor of the Sacred Congregation of the Rites concluded his report with these words: "I pray God that these things become known for the glory of God, and to strengthen the faith of diffident and timid souls, and also that the holy religious of the Sacred Heart who wrote them may be glorified." (Translation from the Italian).

The essence of the message is love and mercy. Nowhere is it fully stated, but it is found in fragmentary form all through the book. Here is a summary of the major points.

a) In the first place, the Sacred Heart and the *overwhelming charity* of Jesus for mankind are brought out in a striking way. It might also be called a new revelation of the Sacred Heart, confirming and in certain matters completing and perfecting that previously given to St. Margaret Mary.

b) Secondly, in order that men be attracted, the Sacred Heart manifests through Josefa his *infinite mercy*: he loves them, every one, just as they are, even the most despicable, even the greatest sinners.

c) Thirdly, *to consecrated souls, Jesus offers a share of his redemptive life.* He asks of all the spirit of sacrifice in love.

d) Finally, he repeatedly offers to all *the thought of his passion,* for it is the sign of his immense love for mankind and the sole hope of salvation.*

This, then, is the story of a fantastic relationship between the simple little Spanish nun and the supernatural powers: a cosmic battle, an almost daily contact with Christ and his Mother, an occasional visitation by St. Madeleine Sophie Barat, and such a direct participation in the passion of Christ that the young sister died, totally spent, at the age of thirty-three.

---

*The facts concerning the "Message" are taken from an introduction to "The Way of Divine Love" by H. Monier Vinard, S.J.

How much credence should we give this story? It may seem excessively pious, inhumanly cruel, the constant torture of an innocent soul offered up as a victim of love. Yet, there is nothing here that offends in the least the fundamental principles of Christian theology. On the contrary, there is a strength and beauty in these revelations that has the same flavor as the Gospel stories.

All along, Josefa was under the supervision of well-informed priests: her confessor in Spain, Father R. F. Rubio; her spiritual director in Les Feuillants, Father Boyer, O.P. Everything she wrote was handed over immediately to the Mother Superior or Assistant Superior of Les Feuillants who witnessed her ecstasies, her abductions, buffetings and burnings by evil spirits. The Bishop of Poitiers, Msgr. Durfort, was kept informed. He had several conversations with Josefa and supported her warmly. As we have seen, her writings were checked by the Mother General in Rome, and endorsed by Cardinal Pacelli and a Consultor of the Sacred Congregation of Rites. It seems therefore perfectly reasonable to accept the Message as authentic. As always, it must be judged by its fruits — which seem to be nothing but edification, holiness and peace.

The Way of Divine Love — Excerpts

June 23, 1920 — During the heavenly moments I spent in that wound (of the Sacred Heart), Jesus gave me to understand that he is rewarding me for the very little I have done to prove my fidelity. I will never again seek my own interests, but only the glory of his Heart. I will try to be very obedient and very generous in the smallest details, for I believe perfection consists in this, and that is the one way straight to him.

July 15, 1920 — He drew me into his heart, and a stream of the precious blood escaping from it submerged me. "For all that you give me," he said, "I give you my Heart."

I believed I was no longer on this earth. He was clothed in

white, and this made his sacred Heart stand out in an ineffable manner. . . .His face was like the sun. . . .O my God, what beauty! How entrancing to those who know you!

"My God, I am yours for ever!" — And I went so far as to babble nonsense in my love. Then he answered: "I, too, Josefa, love you to folly!"

October 17, 1920 — "Always remember that if I love you, it is because you are little, not because you are good."

(In the evening of October 23, 1920, Josefa was on the third floor of the convent, closing some windows.) Suddenly, as I was reaching the passage on the top floor, I saw Jesus coming to meet me from the other end. He was surrounded with light so radiant, so lovely it lit up an otherwise dark passage. He walked rapidly, as if eager to meet me.

"Where do you come from?"

"I have been closing the windows, Lord."

"And where are you going?"

"I am going to finish doing so, my Jesus."

"That is not the way to answer, Josefa."

I did not understand what he meant, and he continued:

"I come from love and I go to love. Whether you go up or down, you are ever in my heart, for it is an abyss of love. I am with you."

(This exquisite little incident is remembered at Poitiers, for the dark passage goes by the name of the Corridor of Love.)

October 20, 1920 — Jesus said: "When I leave you so cold, I am using your warmth to give heat to other souls. When I leave you a prey to anguish, your suffering wards off divine justice as it is about to strike sinners. When it seems to you as if you did not love me, and yet you tell me unceasingly that you do, then you console my heart most. That is what I want: that you should be ready to console my heart every time I need you."

(Josefa's vocation as a victim-soul is slowly being prepared.)

November 8, 1920 — "One single act of love in the loneliness in which I leave you makes up for many of the acts of ingratitude of which I am the object. My heart counts and collects these acts of your love as a precious balm.''

November 20, 1920 — ''Many souls believe love consists in saying, 'My God, I love you!' No, love is sweet, and acts because it loves, and everything it does is done out of love. I want you to love me in that way, in work, in rest, in prayer and consolation as in distress and humiliation, constantly giving proofs of your love by acts. That is true love.''

November 26, 1920 — I was in the little chapel of St. Stanislaus. He was asking me to comfort him and I was thinking about what I could do. ''I will leave you my crown of thorns for a few minutes, Josefa, and you will see what my suffering is.''

At that instant, I felt my head encircled with thorns which pierced deeply into it. Many times this same pain was renewed. So terrible was it that I was about to complain, but he said: ''Do not complain, for nothing will cure you of this pain: it is a share in my sufferings.''

December 4, 1920 — ''I shall be your torment, Josefa, and you shall be my repose. As a traveler along the way occasionally seeks a shelter where he may rest, just such a shelter are you to me.''

December 19, 1920 — ''You are suffering in both soul and body because you are the victim of my soul and of my body. How could you not suffer in your heart since I have chosen you to be the victim of my heart? Courage! I can give you no better gift than suffering: it is the same road I trod.''

December 28, 1920 — ''It seems to you that you see nothing, and that you are about to fall into the abyss. As long as you are guided, do you need to see? What you do need is to forget yourself, to abandon your own will and offer no resistance to my plans.''

January 26, 1921 — ''You will suffer to gain souls because you are the chosen victim of my heart — but you will come to no harm because I will not allow it.''

February 25, 1921 — ''Love, and have no fear. I want what

you do not want, but I can do what you cannot do. It is not for you to choose, but to surrender.''

(Josefa never ceased dreading her mission, and the three years to come would be punctuated by the terrors that assailed her every time she was asked to surrender.)

March 11, 1921 — "If you concern yourself with my glory, I will look after you; I will establish my peace in you so that nothing will be able to trouble you; I will set up in your soul the reign of my love and your joy none shall take away from you.''

(On Holy Saturday, March 26, 1921, Jesus repeated to Josefa what he had once said in almost identical terms to St. Margaret Mary.)

"I want to make of your heart an altar on which the fire of my love will burn constantly. That is why I want it pure, and that nothing that can stain it should touch it.''

(On May 26, the foundress of the Society of the Sacred Heart, St. Madeleine Sophie Barat, communicated for the first time with Josefa.)

Today, on the feast of our blessed Mother (not yet canonized at the time), I went into her cell many times to whisper a little prayer to her, and once — I was in my blue apron — I just stood for a moment and said, "O Mother, once more I ask you to make me very humble, that I may be your true daughter.'' There was no one in the room and this little invocation was said aloud. Suddenly, I became aware of the presence of a nun I did not know. She took my head between her hands and pressed it lovingly, saying, "My child, commit all your frailties to the heart of Jesus, love the heart of Jesus and be faithful to the heart of Jesus.''

I took her hand to kiss it, then with two fingers she made the sign of the cross in blessing on my forehead and disappeared.

June 30, 1921 — "The greatest reward I can give a soul is to make her a victim of my love and mercy, rendering her like myself who am the divine Victim for sinners.''

For the last fifteen or twenty days, my soul has had a sort of attraction for suffering. It used to frighten me, and when Jesus told me he had chosen me as his victim, my whole being quivered. Now it is different. There are days, of course, when the pain is so great that unless he sustained me I could not bear it and survive, for not a single member of my body is spared. Yet my soul longs to bear more, were it possible, though not without resistance in my lower nature. When I begin to feel these pains coming on, I tremble and instinctively recoil — but there is strength in my will that accepts, that determines and desires to suffer more, so that if at that moment I were given the choice between going to heaven or continuing to suffer, I should infinitely prefer to remain on earth that I might console his heart, although I am burning to go to him. I know it is Jesus who has effected this transformation in me and that he is tenderly concerned about me, and this makes me very happy and grateful.

July 8, 1921 — "When you are in pain, I rest, and my heart rejoices in converse with you. Have no fear, for my visits will never harm you; you are in my hands and I will guard you provided you refuse me nothing."

(On January 12, 1922, during her thanksgiving after communion, Jesus became manifest to Josefa.)

I asked him if the trial was over.

"I want you to surrender yourself either to suffering or to rejoicing, and to be always ready to undergo the torments of the evil one, or to receive my consolations — indifferently."

February 13, 1922 — "Come: there is no need to fear, it is I."

Uncertain whether it were really the Lord [for the devil had occasionally appeared to her under the form of Christ], I went to tell the Mothers, and proceeded from there to the tribune where I found him already waiting.

"Yes, Josefa, it is truly I, the Son of the Immaculate Virgin."

Never would the devil, in spite of his effrontery, have dared to use such words.

"Lord, my only love," I answered, "if it be you, deign to

allow me to renew in your presence the vow I have taken for your sake.''

He listened to me with pleasure, and when I had finished, he said: ''Tell your superiors that because you have been faithful to do my will, I too will be faithful to you. Tell them that this trial is over, and oh, what glory it has given to my heart! And you, Josefa (he stretched out his arms and drew me close to his heart), rest in me in peace as I reposed in your sufferings.''

(Between February 14 and March 3, 1922, Josefa enjoyed a period of happiness and consolation, but she was told this was not to last.)

February 14, 1922 — ''All this sweetness is nothing compared with the balm your sufferings were to me, your submission and abandonment to my will. Do not believe I love you more now that I am consoling you than when I ask you to suffer.'' Then, after a brief silence, ''In any case, I cannot leave you without suffering, but your soul must remain in peace, even in the midst of pain.''

March 16, 1922 — In the night of March 16, about ten o'clock, I became aware as on the preceding days of a confused noise of cries and chains. I rose quickly and dressed, and trembling with fright, knelt down near my bed. The uproar was approaching, and not knowing what to do, I left the dormitory and went to our Holy Mother's cell, then came back to the dormitory. The same terrifying sounds were all around me. Then all of a sudden I saw before me the devil himself.

''Tie her feet and bind her hands,'' he cried.

Instantly, I lost sight of where I was and felt myself being tightly bound and dragged away. Other voices screamed, ''No good to bind her feet: it is her heart you must bind!''

''It does not belong to me,'' came the answer from the devil.

Then I was forced along a very dark and long passageway. On all sides terrible cries resounded. On both walls of the narrow corridor were niches out of which poured smoke, though with very little flame, but an intolerable stench. From these recesses came blasphemous voices uttering obscenities. Some cursed their bodies, others their parents, others again reproached themselves for having refused grace and not avoided what they had known to be sinful. It was a medley of confusing screams of rage and despair. I was dragged all along that passage which seemed endless.

Then I received a violent blow which doubled me up and forced me into one of the niches. I felt as though I were being pressed between two burning boards and pierced through and through with red hot needles. Opposite and beside me souls were blaspheming and cursing me. What caused the deepest suffering — no torture can be compared with it — was my soul's anguish at finding myself separated from God.

It seemed I spent long years in that hell, yet the elapsed time was no more than six or seven hours. Suddenly, I was pulled out of the niche, and I found myself in a dark place. After striking me, the devil disappeared and left me free. How can I describe my feelings on realizing I was still alive and could still love God!

(The agony endured by Josefa in those cruel moments seems to have been the ransom of souls she did not know, but whose name, date and place of death she noted. They were verified more than once.)

August 6, 1922 — (The following words, instead of being recorded from memory, were actually dictated to Josefa.) "When you write, I will tell you what you have to say. None of my words will be lost. Nothing I tell you will ever be blotted out. It is of little import that you are so worthless and wretched, for it is I who will do everything.

"I will make it known that my work rests on nothingness and misery: such is the first link in the chain of love I have prepared for souls from all eternity. I will use you to show that I love misery, littleness and absolute nothingness.

"I will reveal to souls the excess of my love and how far I will go in forgiveness, and how even their faults will be used by me with blind indulgence — yes, write *with blind indulgence.* I see the very depths of souls, I see how they would please, console and glorify me, and the act of humility they are obliged to make when they see themselves so weak is a solace and glory to my heart. What does their helplessness matter? I will show how my heart uses their very weakness to give life to many souls that have lost it.

"I will make it known that the measure of my love and mercy for fallen souls is limitless. I want to forgive them. It rests me to forgive. I am ever there, waiting, with boundless love till souls come to me. Let them come, and not be discouraged. Let them throw themselves into my arms fearlessly: I am their Father!

"Many of my religious do not understand how much they can do to draw into my heart those steeped in ignorance. They do not know how much I yearn to attract them to myself and give them life. . . true life.

"Yes, Josefa, I will teach you the secrets of my love, and you will be a living example of my mercy, for if I have such love and predilection for you who are worthless, what am I not ready to do for others more generous than you are?"

(The days went by, leaving Josefa expectant, not knowing what her Master would do. A few days later, she was again summoned to write under dictation.)

August 29, 1922 — "I know the very depth of souls, their passions, their attraction to the world and its pleasures; I have known from all eternity how many of them will fill my heart with bitterness, and that for a great number both my sufferings and my blood will be in vain. But having loved them, I love them still. My heart is not so much wounded by sin as torn by grief — because they will not seek refuge with me after their misdeeds.

"I want to forgive, I want the world to know through my chosen ones that my heart is overflowing with love and mercy, and is waiting for sinners."

September 3, 1922 — *(After communion, Josefa again saw the Lord. He shone with incomparable beauty, and resting his eyes on the nuns who were deep in thanksgiving, he said:)*

"I am enthroned in hearts I have myself prepared. My consecrated ones cannot possibly realize how greatly they relieve the sorrow of my heart by giving me entry into theirs. No doubt they are small and wretched, but they belong to no one but me. Their wretchedness I willingly overlook, for all I want is their love. Weakness and worthlessness are of small account: what I want is their trust. These are the souls who draw down mercy and peace upon the world. Were it not for them, divine justice would hardly be restrained, there is so much sin!"

September 13, 1922 — "Many are willing to entertain me when I visit them with consolations; many receive me with joy in holy communion, but few welcome me when I visit them with my cross. When a soul is stretched out on the cross and surrenders to my will, it glorifies me and consoles me and is very close to me."

October 20, 1922 — "The world is full of perils. How many poor souls are dragged towards sin and constantly need a visible or invisible help! Ah, let me say it again: do my chosen souls know of what treasures they are depriving themselves and others when they are ungenerous? I do not say that a soul is freed from her faults and her wretchedness because chosen by me: that soul may and will fall often again — but if she humbles herself, if she acknowledges her nothingness, if she tries to repair her faults by small deeds of generosity and love, if she confides and surrenders herself once more to my heart, she gives me more glory and can do more good to other souls than if she had never fallen. Miseries and weaknesses are of no consequence: what I do ask of them is love. But, Josefa, you must realize I am speaking only of faults of frailty and inadvertence — not of willed sin or intended infidelity."

(Josefa then expressed her fears in the face of the many graces and responsibilities she had received.)

"Do not fear: if I have chosen you who are poor and wretched, it is so that all may realize once more that I want neither greatness nor holiness, but only love. I myself will do all the rest. And I will again tell you the secrets of my heart, Josefa, but the desire which consumes me is ever the same: it is that souls may know my heart better and better.''

November 23, 1922 — ''I will begin by speaking to my chosen souls, and to all who are consecrated to me. They must know me so as to be able to teach those I shall confide to their care all the kindness and tenderness of my heart, and to tell all that if I am an infinitely just God, I am nonetheless an infinitely merciful Father. Let my chosen souls, my spouses, my religious and priests, teach all poor souls how much I love them! All this I will teach you by degrees, and thus I shall be glorified in your abjection, in your littleness, in your nothingness. I do not love you for what you are, but for what you are not, that is to say, your wretchedness and nothingness, for thus I have found a place for my greatness and bounty. . . .I wish to be served in joy of heart, but do not forget the nothingness of the instrument. . . .

''You cannot conceive how great is the reparatory value of suffering. . . .One act of abandonment glorifies me more than many sacrifices.''

November 28, 1922 — ''I am all love! My heart is an abyss of love.

''It was love that made man and all existing things that they might be at his service.

''It was love that moved the Father to give his Son for man's salvation which through his own fault he had lost.

''It was love that caused a Virgin who was little more than a child to renounce the charms of life in the Temple and consent to become the Mother of God, thereby accepting all the suffering involved in the divine Maternity.

''It was love that caused me to be born in the inclemency of winter, poor and destitute of everything.

''It was love that hid me thirty years in complete obscurity and humble work.

''It was love that made me choose solitude and silence: to live unknown and voluntarily to submit to the commands of my mother and adopted father. For love saw how in the course of ages many souls would follow my example and delight in conforming their lives to mine.

"It was love that made me embrace all the miseries of human nature, for the love of my heart saw far ahead. I knew how many imperiled souls would be helped by the acts and sacrifices of others and so would recover life.

"It was love that made me suffer the most ignominious contempt and horrible tortures, and to shed all my blood and die on the cross to save mankind and redeem the whole human race.

"And love saw how, in the future, many souls would unite themselves to my torments and dye their sufferings and actions, even the most ordinary, with my blood in order to win many souls to me.

"I will teach you all this very clearly, Josefa, that men may know how far-reaching is the love of my heart for them.

"And now go back to your work and live in me as I do in you."

November 30, 1922 — "The soul who constantly unites her life with mine glorifies me and does a great deal of work for others. While engaged in work of no intrinsic value, she may bathe it in my blood or unite it to the work I myself did during my mortal life. This will greatly profit souls, more perhaps than if she had preached to the whole world — and that, whether she studies, speaks or writes, whether she sews, sweeps or rests, provided first that the act be sanctioned by obedience or duty and not done from mere caprice; secondly, that it be done in intimate union with me, with great purity of intention and covered with my blood.

"I so much want souls to understand this! It is not the action in itself that is of value; it is the intention with which it is done. When I swept and labored in the workshop of Nazareth, I gave as much glory to my Father as when I preached during my public life.

"There are many souls who in the eyes of the world fill important posts and they give my heart great glory; this is true. But I have many hidden souls who in their humble labors are very useful laborers in my vineyard, for they are moved by love and they know how to cover their deeds with supernatural gold by bathing them in my blood. My love goes so far that my souls can draw great treasure out of mere nothing. When as soon as they wake they unite themselves to me and offer their whole day with a burning desire that my heart may use it for the profit of souls, when they perform their duties with love, hour by hour and moment by moment, how great is the treasure they amass in one day!

"I will reveal my love to them more and more: it is inexhaustible, and how easy it is for a loving soul to let herself be guided by love!"

December 2, 1922 — "My heart is all love and it embraces all souls, but how can I make my chosen souls understand my special love for them and how I wish to use them to save sinners and so many souls who are exposed to the perils of the world? For this reason, I would like them to know how much I desire their perfection, and that it consists in doing their ordinary actions in intimate union with me. If they once grasped this, they could divinize their lives and all their activities by this close union with my heart — and how great is the value of a divinized day!

"When a soul is consumed with a desire to love, nothing is a burden to her, but if she feels cold and spiritless, everything becomes hard and difficult. Let her then come to my heart to revive her courage. Let her offer me her dejection, and unite it to my fervor; then she may rest content, for her day will be of incomparable value to souls. All human miseries are known to my heart and my compassion for them is great.

"But I desire souls to unite themselves to me not only in a general way: I long for this union to be constant and intimate as it is between friends who live together; for even if they are not talking all the time, at least they look at each other, and their mutual affectionate little kindnesses are the fruit of their love.

"When a soul is in peace and consolation, doubtless it is easier for her to think of me, but if she is in the throes of desolation and anguish, she need not fear: I am content with a glance. I understand, and this mere look will draw down on her special signs of my tenderness.

"I will repeat again to souls how much my heart loves them, for I want them to know me thoroughly, that they may make me known to those I place in their care.

"I ardently desire my chosen souls to fix their eyes on me, and never turn them away; and among them there should be no mediocrity, which usually is the result of a misunderstanding of my love. No! It is neither difficult nor hard to love my heart, but on the contrary, it is sweet and easy. They need do nothing extraordinary to attain to a high degree of love: purity of intention — be the action great or small — intimate union with my heart, and love will do the rest."

December 5, 1922 — "My heart is not only an abyss of love, it is also an abyss of mercy; and knowing as I do that even my closest friends are not exempt from human frailties, I want each of their actions, however insignificant, to be clothed through me with immense value for the help of those in need and for the salvation of sinners.

"All cannot preach or evangelize distant uncivilized peoples. But all, yes, all can make my heart known and loved. All can mutually help one another to increase the number of the saved by preventing the loss of many souls — and that, through my love and mercy.

"I will tell my chosen souls that my love for them goes further still; not only shall I make use of their daily lives and of their least actions, but I will make use of their very wretchedness, their frailties, even of their falls, for the salvation of souls.

"Love transforms and divinizes everything, and mercy pardons all."

December 12, 1922 — "Souls that see themselves overwhelmed with miseries attribute nothing good to themselves, and their very abjectness clothes them with a certain humility they would not have had if they had seen themselves to be less imperfect.

"When, therefore, in the course of apostolic work or in the carrying out of duties, a consciousness of their incapacity is forced upon them, or when they experience a kind of repugnance to helping souls towards perfections to which they know themselves to be still strangers, such souls are compelled to humble themselves in the dust, and should this self-knowledge impel them to my feet, asking pardon for their halting efforts, begging of my heart the strength and courage they need, it is hardly possible for them to conceive how lovingly my heart goes out to them and how marvelously fruitful I will make their labors.

"Those whose generosity is not equal to these daily endeavors and sacrifices will see their lives go by, full only of promise which will never come to fruition.

"But in this, distinguish: to souls who habitually promise and yet do no violence to themselves nor prove their abnegation and love in any way, I say: 'Beware lest all this straw and stubble which you have gathered into your barns take fire or be scattered in an instant by the wind!'

"But there are others, and it is of them that I now speak, who begin their day with a very good will and desire to prove their love. They pledge themselves to self-denial or generosity in this or that circumstance. But when the time comes, they are prevented by self-love, temperament, health, or I know not what, from carrying out what a few hours before they quite sincerely purposed to do. Nevertheless they speedily acknowledge their weakness and, filled with shame, beg for pardon, humble themselves, and renew their promise. Ah! let them know that they please me as much as if they had nothing to blame themselves for."

February 11, 1923 — "This should be your constant prayer, Josefa: 'Eternal Father, who out of love for mankind gave up your beloved Son to death, by his blood, by his merits, by his heart, have pity on the whole world, and forgive all the sins that are there committed. Receive the humble reparation offered to you by your chosen souls. Unite it to the merits of your divine Son, so that all they do may be very effective. O eternal Father, have pity on souls, and remember that the time has not yet come for strict justice, but for mercy.' ''

(During the Lent of 1923, the Lord gave Josefa an hour by hour account of his thoughts from the time of the Washing of the Feet until his Death on the Cross. Although the narrative is extraordinarily moving, it is too long to fit within the framework of the present study. Rather than offer truncated fragments, we prefer to direct the reader to the complete text in Josefa's official biography, "The Way of Divine Love.")

May 20, 1923 — ''Josefa, do you not know that I and the cross are inseparable? If you meet me, you meet the cross, and when you find the cross, it is me you have found. Whoever loves me loves the cross, and whoever loves the cross loves me. Only those who love the cross and embrace it willingly for love of me, will possess eternal life. The path of virtue and of holiness is composed of abnegation and suffering. Whoever generously accepts the cross walks in true light, follows a straight and sure path, with no danger from steep inclines down which to slide, for there are none there.

''My cross is the door of true life, that is why it is illuminated. And the soul that knows how to accept and love it, just as I have chosen it for her, will enter by it into the glory of life eternal.

''Do you now understand how precious the cross is? Do not shun it: love it, for it comes from me, and I shall never leave you without the strength to bear it. I bore it for love of you: will you not bear it for love of me?''

(Jesus now resumes his message of love, speaking in words Josefa is to hand over to the Bishop of Poitiers.)

June 11, 1923 — ''I am *Love*! My heart can no longer contain its devouring flames. I love souls so dearly that I have sacrificed my life for them.

''It is this love that keeps me a prisoner in the tabernacle. For nearly twenty centuries I have dwelt there, night and day, veiled under the species of bread and concealed in the small white host, bearing, through love, neglect, solitude, contempt, blasphemies, outrages, sacrileges.

"For love of souls I instituted the Sacrament of Penance, that I might forgive them, not once or twice, but as often as they need to recover grace. There I wait for them, longing to wash away their sins, not in water, but in my blood.

"How often in the course of the ages have I, in one way or another, made known my love for men: I have shown them how ardently I desire their salvation. I have revealed my heart to them. This devotion has been as light cast over the whole earth, and today it is a powerful means of gaining souls, and so of extending my kingdom.

"Now I want something more, for if I long for love in response to my own, this is not the only return I desire from souls: I want them all to have confidence in my mercy, to expect all from my clemency, and never to doubt my readiness to forgive.

"I am God, but a God of love! I am a Father, but a Father full of compassion and never harsh. My heart is infinitely holy, but also infinitely wise. And knowing human frailty and infirmity, it stoops to poor sinners with infinite mercy.

"I love those who after a first fall come to me for pardon. I love them still more when they beg pardon for their second sin, and should this happen again, I do not say a million times but a million million times, I still love them and pardon them, and I will wash in my blood their last sin as fully as their first.

"Never shall I weary of repentant sinners, nor cease from hoping for their return. And the greater their distress, the greater my welcome. Does not a father love a sick child with special affection? Are not his care and solicitude greater? So is the tenderness and the compassion of my heart more abundant for sinners than for the just.

"This is what I wish all to know. I will teach sinners that the mercy of my heart is inexhaustible. Let the callous and indifferent know that my heart is a fire which will enkindle them, because I love them. To devout and saintly souls I would be the Way, that, making great strides in perfection, they may safely reach the harbor of eternal beatitude. Lastly, of consecrated souls,. priests and religious, my elect and chosen ones, I ask once more all their love and that they should not doubt mine, but above all that they should trust me and never doubt my mercy. It is so easy to trust completely in my heart!''

June 12, 1923 — "I want to forgive, I want to reign over souls and pardon all nations. I want to rule souls, nations, the whole world. My peace must be extended over the entire universe, but in a special way over this dear country where devotion to my heart first took root. Oh, that I might be its Peace, its Life, its King! I am Wisdom and Beatitude; I am Love and Mercy! I am Peace; I shall reign! I will shower my mercies on the world to wipe out its ingratitude. To make reparation for its crimes, I will choose victims who will obtain pardon, for there are in the world many whose desire is to please me, and there are moreover generous souls who will sacrifice everything they possess, that I may use them according to my will and good pleasure.

"My reign shall be one of peace and love and I shall inaugurate it by compassion on all. Such is the end I have in view and this is the great work of my love.

"It is *founded* on love. Its *end* is love. Its *life* is love — and what is love but my heart?

"As for you, I have chosen you as a useless and incapable being, so that it may be clearly I who speak, who ask, who act.

"My appeal is addressed to all: to those consecrated in religion and to those living in the world, to the good and to sinners, to the learned and to the illiterate, to those in authority and to those who obey. To each of them I come to say: if you seek happiness you will find it in me; if riches, I am infinite Wealth; if you desire peace, in me alone is Peace to be found. I am Mercy and Love and I must be sovereign King.

"This is what you will give the bishop to read. . . .Let him not be surprised at the kind of instrument I use, for my power is infinite and self-sufficient. Let him trust me. I will bless his undertakings. And now, Josefa, I shall begin to speak directly to the world, and I desire that my words be made known after your death. As regards yourself, you will live in the most complete anddeepest obscurity, and because I have chosen you as my victim, you will suffer, and overwhelmed with pain, you will die! Do not look for rest or alleviation: you will find none, for so have I disposed things. But my love will uphold you, and never shall I fail you!"

(Once again, Josefa is warned about the mystery of love and suffering. That the greatest Love would procure the greatest suffering followed by an early death is the unfathomable secret of divine providence.

(During the following days, Jesus addressed an appeal to mankind, in the form of a parable about a man who sent his only son to heal the servants he loved. Here again, as in the case of the Passion, the text is splendid and moving. It cannot be summarized, nor do we have the space to reproduce it in full. This "message to the world" lasted until June 20, 1923. Then followed a long period when the Lord no longer appeared to Josefa, while the devil once again was permitted to persecute her. On the 16th of July, she again enjoyed a radiant day of grace.

(This was followed by a new period of trials, from July 16 to August 24, 1923, interspersed with visits from St. John the Evangelist and the Mother of God. Jesus appeared, too, giving her instructions for the bishop, whom she met several times. Periods of light and darkness alternated until the first day of June, 1923, when she was sent to Rome, ostensibly as a servant to the Superiors on retreat there, though in fact, as a result of an order she had received from the Mother of God to give a full report to the Mother

Superior of the Society. During the trip to Rome, Jesus appeared to Josefa:)

October 2, 1923 — ". . .Remember these words: 'I work in darkness, yet I am light.' I have warned you more than once that the day will come when everything will seem lost, and my great work brought to nothing. But today I tell you, 'The light will return, stronger than ever.' "

(Josefa returned to Poitiers on October 26. The Lord appeared to her again. Then from October 28 to November 13, she did not see him. On the 13th, Jesus dictated a new message for the bishop.)

November 13, 1923 — "I desire that my love should be the sun to enlighten, and the heat to reanimate souls. That is why my words must reach them. I want all the world to recognize in me a God of mercy and of love. I wish that everywhere my desire to forgive and save souls should be read, and that not even the most wretched be kept back by fear, nor the most guilty fly from me. Let them all come. I await them with open arms like the most affectionate of fathers in order to impart life and true happiness to them.

"That the world may know my clemency, I need apostles who will reveal my heart, but first these must know it themselves, otherwise how can they teach?

"So for the next few days I will speak for my priests, my religious and my nuns, that all may clearly understand what I require: I want them to form a league of love in order to teach and publish the love and mercy of my heart to all men, even to the extremities of the world. I want the need and desire for reparation to be re-awakened and grow among faithful and chosen souls, for the world is full of sin, and at this present moment nations are arousing the wrath of God. But he desires his reign to be one of love, hence this appeal to chosen souls, especially those of this nationality. He asks them to repair, to obtain pardon, and above all to draw down grace on this country which was the first to know my heart and spread devotion to it.

"I want the world to be saved, peace and union to prevail

everywhere. It is my will to reign, and reign I shall, through reparation made by chosen souls, and through a new realization by all men of my kindness, my mercy and my love.

"My words will be light and life for an incalculable number of souls. They will all be printed, read and preached, and I will grant a very special grace, that by them souls may be enlightened and transformed."

December 4, 1923 — "I wish to speak today to my consecrated religious, that they may make me known to sinners and to the whole world.

"There are many among them who as yet are unable to understand my true feelings. They treat me as one far away, known only slightly, and in whom they have too little confidence. I want them to rekindle their faith and love, and live trustfully in my intimacy, loving and loved.

"It is usually the eldest son of the family who knows best the mind and secret affairs of his father. In him the father is wont to confide more than in the younger ones, who as yet are unable to interest themselves in serious matters, or penetrate below the surface of things. So when the father comes to die, it behooves the eldest brother to transmit his wishes and will to these the younger ones.

"In my Church, too, I have elder sons: they are those whom I myself have chosen, consecrated by the priesthood or by the vows of religion. They live nearest to me; they share in my choicest graces, and to them I confide my secrets, my desires, and my sufferings also. I have committed to them the care of my little children, their brothers, and through their ministry they must, directly or indirectly, guide them and transmit my teachings to them. . . ."

(Instructions such as these are continued until the last page of Josefa's diary, dated December 9, 1923. It seems that after that, she was too weak to write.)

December 8, 1923 — This evening, while I was in the chapel, suddenly Our Blessed Lady came. She was clothed in her usual attire, but surrounded with dazzling light and standing on a crescent of azure blue clouds which were very airy and ethereal. On her head she wore a long, pale blue veil, transparent as gossamer, which was lost in the clouds on which her feet rested. She was so lovely that I dared say nothing to her. My soul melted as I gazed on her beauty.

At last, I managed to renew my vows, and she said to me in a voice both sweet and grave: "My child, the Church honors me today by contemplating my Immaculate Conception. Men admire in me the wonders wrought by God, and the beauty with which he clothed me even before original sin could stain my soul. He who is the Eternal God chose me for his Mother and overwhelmed my soul with graces greater than any bestowed on any creature. All the beauty you see in me is a reflection of the divine perfections, and the praises given me glorify him who, being my Creator, willed to make me his Mother.

"My choicest title to glory is that of being immaculate at the same time as being Mother of God. But my greatest joy is to add to this title that of Mother of Mercy, and Mother of Sinners."

When she had said this, she vanished, and I have not seen her again.

(Here end Josefa's notes.)

VI

CONCEPCIÓN CABRERA
DE ARMIDA (Conchita)

CONCEPCIÓN CABRERA DE ARMIDA
(Conchita)(1862-1937)

The other women mystics covered in the present book are all Europeans. Here at last we meet a true daughter of North America. Born on December 8, 1862 in San Luis Potosi, Mexico, she became a social butterfly, sought in marriage by many suitors. On November 8, 1884, she married Francisco Armida who died on September 7, 1901, leaving her a widow with eight children. Although her marriage had been good, she grieved for never having revealed to her husband the secret of her soul.

Since the age of nineteen, she had been filled with an intense desire for perfection, progressively leading to the experience of spiritual marriage on Febraury 9, 1897. For over forty years, she kept a Spiritual Diary which amounted to sixty-six hand-written volumes.

As to the authenticity of her works, besides the warm support of her countless followers and of the members of the two religious orders she founded, we have the testimony of a special commission established in Rome in 1913, one member of which concluded: "She is extraordinary of the extraordinary!" His Eminence Miguel Dario Cardinal Miranda, Archbishop-Primate of Mexico introduced her published works with a letter of unqualified support. Her process of beatification and canonization has been introduced in Rome.

A French Dominican priest, Father M.M. Philipon, assumed the gigantic task of presenting Conchita's work to the general public. He died before completing his task, which was taken over

by Father Roberto de la Rosa, Missionary of the Holy Spirit, a
member of the religious order for men which Conchita had
founded.

There is a very unusual balance in Conchita's life. While
knowing perfectly well that she was called to the heights of mystical experience, she managed to live her natural life to the full and to
maintain a perfect harmony between the two callings.

"My betrothal never troubled me as an obstacle to my belonging to God. It seemed to me so easy to combine them both!" Her
life was filled with the usual hardships of motherhood, the labors
and diseases, even the loss of a ninth child, a son who died of
typhoid fever at the age of six. Very early on she had been warned:

> The Lord told me: "The world is buried in sensuality, no
> longer is sacrifice loved and no longer is its sweetness known.
> I wish the Cross to reign. Today it is presented to the world
> with my Heart, so that it may bring souls to make sacrifices.
> No true love is without sacrifice. It is only in my crucified
> Heart that the ineffable sweetness of my Heart can be tasted.
> Seen from the outside, the Cross is bitter and harsh, but as
> soon as tasted, penetrating and savoring it, there is no greater
> pleasure. Therein is the repose of the soul, the soul inebriated
> by love, therein its delights, its life" (p. 33 — *Aut.* I:216/
> 218).

In the very first volume of her autobiographical notes, she
records her immersion in the Christian paradox of suffering.

> The Lord told me: "Do not complain about your suffer-
> ings before strangers. Do not let them see how you are in pain:
> that would lessen your merit. Suffer in silence. Let me work
> in you and walk the earth silently and obscurely crucified"
> (*Diary,* April 1898).

The experiences of suffering are more than compensated by
moments of extraordinary illumination:

The Lord unrolled before me spiritual panoramas which left me mute in admiration. Suddenly I found myself involved in the most profound secrets of the spiritual life. I contemplated its ravishing beauties, its formidable abysses, its delights and dangers. I do not know for what purpose and in what manner he conducted me in these so unknown areas. . . .Why do these flashes of interior light burst out in me at any moment at all? Why do the supernatural and the divine present themselves to me so clearly? At times I think that all this is purely natural and within the range of my intelligence, but I know the rudeness and limitations of my spirit and I cannot but admit that such illuminations are extraordinary and graces from heaven, even though I do not know their purpose (*Diary,* March 21, 1901).

When Conchita believes her mystical experiences may be natural, she is in the tradition of other mystics, for instance, St. Bonaventure of Bagnorea:

There are two roads to truth: the simply rational which proceeds by way of abstraction from sense experience, and the mystical which proceeds by way of intuition or inner apprehension. The first is the natural way, the second, the supernatural. If Bonaventure seems to accept both as natural, it is all to his praise; it is a sign of so deep an immersion in the supernatural that this way, special as it is, appeared to him as being open to all.*

Some time before Conchita's definitive experience of mystical marriage, she was already receiving profound revelations on the nature of the Trinity. God was speaking to her:

"Eternally *I am*: *I am* covers all eternity. For me, there exists neither before nor after, neither past nor future. I cannot say *I have been* or *I shall be,* but eternally *I am.*"

---

*Introduction, *The Works of Bonaventure,* Vol. II, tl. José de Vinck, St. Anthony Guild, Paterson, 1963.

"Why do you tell me this, Lord, if I do not understand it?"

"Before creation, at the bottom of my eternal Being, without beginning, I AM now. . . . I AM eternally. I AM by my very self. Nothing was brought to me. I bear in me all the perfections and attributes which I produce from my own essence. I am blessed because I am eternal, ever enjoying within my own self eternal Truth: Father, Son and Holy Spirit, the Whole in Unity, three Persons in one single substance, there is your God thrice Holy! Holy! Holy!"

And I, in truth, am confused. I cannot think or reason, and then feel I am at such heights I can but lower myself into the bottomless abyss of my nothingness. I close my eyes. I believe and I adore. . . ! (*Diary*, August 8, 1896)

Here is a confession of humility combined with the most sublime and orthodox teaching on the nature of the Trinity. Some time later, Christ himself confirms and completes this teaching:

The Lord next elevated my spirit to a contemplation of the Incarnation of the Word. He made me understand most profound things in relation to the Most Holy Trinity of which he is the Second Person.

The Lord told me: "My Father existed from all eternity. He produced from the depth of himself, of his own substance, of his very essence, his Word. From all eternity too, from the beginning, already there was the Word-God and the Father who is God, the two Persons constituting but one same divine substance. But never, at any moment, were these divine Persons, the Father and the Son, alone or only two. In this same eternity, but inspired by the Father and the Son, the Holy Spirit existed, reflection, substance, essence of the Father and the Son, and equally Person. The Holy Trinity is a divine reflection in the bosom of the same divinity, the reflection of Love in the bosom of Love itself. The Holy Spirit is the reflection of Light in the bosom of Light itself, the reflection of Life within Life itself, and likewise, of all the infinite perfections in the most intimate depths of eternal perfection. This communication of the same substance, of the same essence, of the same life and of the same perfection which form and are in reality one and the same essence, substance, life and perfection, constitute the eternal felicity of one and the same God and the endless complacencies of the august Trinity" (*Diary*, February 25, 1897).

All along, Conchita was being prepared for her special mission, a sacrificial priesthood for the salvation of souls. On June 21, 1906, Jesus says to her:

"You will be my altar and at the same time my victim. Offer yourself in union with me, offer me at each moment to the eternal Father, with the so exalted purpose of saving souls and of glorifying him. Forget everything, and above all, forget yourself. Let that be your constant occupation. You have received a sublime mission, the mission of a priest. Admire my bounty and show your gratitude. Without your knowing it, I have given you what you desired so much, and much, much more than that: the ability to be a priest, not that of holding me in your hands but in your heart, and the grace of never separating myself from you. Achieve the grandiose finality of this grace. As you see, it is not for you alone but universal, obliging you with all possible purity to be at one and the same time altar and victim, consumed in holocaust with the other Victim, the sole Host which may be agreeable to God and which may save the world."

Perhaps we have here a solution to the acute problem of women-priests. The important thing, the greater reality is not the physical consecration of the host in the hands, but the spiritual possession of Christ in the heart. This is not to say that in the evolution of the Church there will never be women-priests, but that even as of now, the very essence of priestly service is available to those women who understand and accept Conchita's message. Their state is in no way inferior to that of men, nor are they denied any privilege because of their sex. God is with them as well as with men, and they can offer him as well as any man.

Conchita, in her great humility, was sometimes tempted to doubt the authenticity of the revelations she was receiving. The Lord categorically answered her last doubts:

> "If (what you write) is from me, it will be for my glory; if it is from the devil, you will be warned; if it is from yourself, you will be mocked, and you will profit from this humiliation" (No date given).

At other times, she surrenders to the very human weakness of finding her spiritual burden excessive:

> I would like to stop writing, forget everything, turn the page, change my life. Such is, at this moment, the state of my spirit, submerged in temptations and sufferings. I must control myself, with God's grace. I renounce myself without pity and keep on going, even though I may die in the struggle (*Diary*, March 26, 1897).

The peak of the revelations Conchita received may be seen as the Lord's instructions concerning the doctrine of the Cross:

> "I wish that above all there be honored the interior sufferings of my Heart, sufferings undergone from my incarnation to the Cross and which are mystically prolonged in my Eucharist. These sufferings are still unsuspected by the world. Nonetheless, I declare to you that, from the first moment of my incarnation, the Cross already planted in my heart overburdened me, and the thorns penetrated it. The

blow struck by the lance might have been some solace caus-
ing to gush from my side a volcano of love and of suffering,
but I did not consent to that until after my death. I only
received ingratitude. That is why my Heart, overflowing with
tenderness, will ever feel the thorns of the Cross. In heaven,
as God, I cannot suffer. To find this Cross which above did
not exist, I descended into this world and became man. As
God-Man, I could suffer infinitely to pay the price of the
salvation of so many souls. During my life, I never desired
anything except the Cross, and ever the Cross, wanting to
show the world that which is the sole wealth and happiness on
earth, the currency which will buy an eternal happiness''
(*Diary,* September 25, 1894).

The second major point in Conchita's writings regards the
doctrine of the Holy Spirit:

"There exists a hidden treasure, a treasure remaining
unexploited and in no ways appreciated at its true worth,
which is nevertheless that which is the greatest in heaven and
earth: the Holy Spirit. The world of souls itself does not know
him as it should. He is the Light of intellects and the Fire that
enkindles hearts. If there is indifference, coldness, weakness, and so many other evils which afflict the spiritual world
and even my Church, it is because recourse is not had to the
Holy Spirit.

"His mission in heaven, his life, his being, is Love.

"On earth, his mission consists in leading souls toward
this heart of Love which is God. With him, there is possessed
all that can be desired.

"If there is sadness, it is because recourse is not had to
this divine Consoler, to him who is perfect spiritual joy. If
there is weakness, it is because there is no reliance on him
who is invincible Might. If there are errors, it is because of
disregard for him who is Light. Faith is extinguished through

the absence of the Holy Spirit. In each heart and in the whole Church, there is not rendered the Holy Spirit that which is due to him. Most of the evils that are deplored in the Church and in the field of souls comes from not according to the Holy Spirit the primacy which I have given to this Third Person of the Trinity who has taken so active a part in the incarnation of the Word and in the founding of the Church. He is loved lukewarmly, invoked without fervor, and in many hearts, even among my own, not even called to mind. All this deeply wounds my Heart" (*Diary,* February 19,1911).

On January 26, 1915, she received further revelations on the same subject:

"Some souls think that the Holy Spirit is very far away, far, far, up above. Actually he is, we might say, the divine Person who is most closely present to the creature. He accompanies him everywhere. He penetrates him with himself. He calls him, he protects him. He makes of him his living temple. He defends him. He helps him. He guards him from all his enemies. He is closer to him than his own soul. All the good a soul accomplishes, it carries out under his inspiration, in his light, by his grace and his help. And yet, he is not invoked, he is not thanked for his direct and intimate action in each soul. If you invoke the Father, if you love him, it is through the Holy Spirit. If you love me ardently, if you know me, if you serve me, if you imitate me, if you make yourself but one with my wishes and with my heart, it is through the Holy Spirit" (*Diary,* January 26, 1915).

Still, Conchita is not convinced of God's accessibility, even that of Christ:

"Oh Jesus, if such a distance separates us, if between this nothingness and your Immensity there is an impassable abyss, how is union possible between these two poles?"

"Between these two poles, God and you, I am there. I, God made man, alone can join them very closely. No one arrives at the immensity of God, no one perceives my divinity, without passing through me. Likewise, without me, no one can humble himself, nor be conscious of his nothingness. I am the Center, the Gateway, the Road, the Light which gives self-knowledge and introduces to contemplation. I am the Point of Encounter, the Redeemer, the Light, the Life, the Hearth of eternal perfection. Study this book, your Christ, and you will be a saint on imitating him" (*Diary*, August 25, 1895).

Much later, the humanity of Christ is described in a striking manner:

"I am man. If I had not existed, man would never have existed. God loves the soul as a reflection of the Trinity and he loves the body as a reflection of me, the perfect Man, type and model of every man" (*Diary*, July 27, 1906).

Conchita also was told about the Mother of God.

"She was beautiful with the beauty of God. She was a virgin of the fertile virginity of the Trinity, a creature without the least stain and all perfect, a soul preserved already, from the time of being in the bosom of the Father, called never to be soiled nor even in the slightest way touched by the least shadow of sin. Already from this eternity, she was Daughter, Spouse and Mother, the three divine Persons finding their pleasure in the perfect work which must be marveled at by heaven and earth throughout all ages. What grandeur in Mary, in the multitude of her perfections, but above all in this work of the virginal incarnation of the Word, prepared for from all eternity.

"The Trinity loved passionately this incomparable creature, and that is why the Word became flesh. He prepared her

with all graces and favors of the Holy Spirit, with the prodigality of a God, coming to make of her his living temple''
(*Diary*, July 23, 1906).

''After the Trinity and with my glorious humanity, Mary
is the noblest creature who exists and can exist in heaven, for
God himself, even though divine, cannot bring about anything more worthy, more perfect and more beautiful, since
she bears in her being the reflection of all the perfections God
can communicate to the creature. That is why Mary's glory in
heaven surpasses that of all the angels and of all the saints''
(*Diary*, August 1906).

Conchita herself expresses beautifully the reason for her devotion to Mary:

The measure of sorrow is that of love, the measure of love
is that of grace, and Mary was full of grace, of love and of
sorrow (*Diary*, March 17, 1894).

Jesus goes on to explain Mary's mission:

''Mary lived to give her testimony about me in my humanity, the Holy Trinity testified about my divinity. She
lived to be in some way the visible instrument of the Holy
Spirit in the nascent Church, while the Holy Spirit acted on
the divine and wholly spiritual plane. She lived to provide its
first nourishment for this unique and true Church, and to
merit in heaven the titles of Consoler, Advocate, Refuge of
her children.

''This phase of Mary's life, constituting for her heart a
source of bitterness, the quintessence of martyrdom, the
purification of her love, and at the same time an inexhaustible
source of grace and mercy, has remained unknown'' (*Diary*,
June 30, 1917).

When speaking of the mystery of the Church — another major

theme of Conchita's revelations — Jesus explains to her the meaning of consecration, extending the act of offering to all the faithful:

"When I pronounced these words, 'Do this in memory of me,' I was not addressing myself only to priests. Of course, they alone have the power to change the substance of bread into my most holy body and the substance of wine into my blood. But the power to unite in one single oblation all oblations belongs to all Christians. It belongs to all Christians, members of one single body, to become one with the Victim on the altar by faith and works, offering me as host in propitiation to my eternal Father" (*Diary,* June 7, 1916).

The editors of the *Diary* remark at this point:

More than a thousand pages of her *Diary* are filled with what the Lord confided, pages which at once reveal the grandeur and the weakness of priests. Therein are found pages without precedent in the history of Christian literature. This urgent appeal for priestly holiness, written thirty years before the Council, is the culminating point of Conchita's *prophetic mission* in the Church (*Conchita,* p.197).

"May all at once this Holy Spirit begin to be called on with prayers, penance and tears, with the ardent desire of his coming. He will come. I will send him again clearly manifest in his effects, which will astonish the world and impel the Church to holiness" (*Diary,* September 27, 1918).

"One day not too far away, at the center of my Church, at St. Peter's, there will take place the consecration of the world to the Holy Spirit, and the graces of this divine Spirit will be showered on the blessed pope who will make it" (*Diary,* March 11, 1928).

As a conclusion to this collection of excerpts, we could do no better than to quote the communication Conchita received on April 22, 1913, concerning the mystery of God.

"God could not be alone, although he is unique. He could not maintain himself in only one divine Person, because he is God, that is, infinite, not limited. On account of his infinite might in the order of charity, he had to communicate himself with all his perfections, and this love being such, so intense and infinite, could not be reserved, I might say, to one also wholly divine and infinite Person, in the Father himself, but he had to produce the Word, and if this might of love redoubled itself in the two divine Persons, love had to personify itself in the Holy Spirit, producing then this Being of Charity, this Fire from the same fire burning between the Father and the Son, forming the bond of union which rejoices them, delights them, and which unifies them and reflects in all fullness their perfections.

"The three divine Persons communicate their attributes and perfections which are themselves, forming this unity which is God, and with this word 'God' all is said" (*Diary,* April 22, 1913).

What, then are the major points of Conchita's doctrine?

From the viewpoint of practical life, she insists on the equality of women as regards spiritual favors and the attainment of mystical heights. She is in the great tradition of other women mystics, Teresa of Avila, Catherine of Siena, Gertrude the Great, in that she contributed richly to the dogmatic teachings of the Church. All this may be summarized as follows:

1) Holiness is for all

While there had been a consistent belief in the Church and its followers that sanctity was a privilege of religious celibates, Conchita proves by her very life that it is open as well to the married living in the world. This was confirmed by the Lord himself who told her one day, "You married in view of my great designs for your personal holiness, and to be an *example* for many souls who believe that marriage is *incompatible* with holiness.'' Marriage, as well as the state of consecrated virginity, may be entered with the intention of promoting God's glory in the highest way.

This matter has been clarified once and for all in a letter addressed by Pope Pius XII to Bishop Charue of Namur, Belgium, on July 13, 1952. Bishop Charue had consulted the pope on the question of whether the life of the regular priest was more perfect and generous than that of the secular. The pope answered that, in fact, it is not even more perfect than that of the layman.

Speaking of the state of perfection, the pope writes:

> Thus it is not the personal perfection of the individual which is under consideration. This is measured by the degree of love, of ''theological charity'' which has been reached in him. The criterion of the intensity and purity of love, according to the Master's words, consists in the fulfillment of God's will. Hence the individual is personally all the more perfect before God as he accomplishes more perfectly the divine intentions. In this matter, the state in which he lives is of little importance, be it lay or ecclesiastical, and, for the priest, be it secular or regular.

The same notion is developed in the Constitution *De Ecclesia*:

> All the faithful of Christ, of whatever rank and status, are called to the fullness of Christian life and to the perfection of charity.
> And so, the highest mansions of heaven are open to every human being, for there is no bar to them besides sin, and no condition besides love.*

*Cf. *The Virtue of Sex*, José de Vinck, Alleluia Press

2) *Importance of the Cross*

Perhaps Conchita is at her best when she describes to us the revelations she received concerning the mystery of suffering. She herself experienced it in many ways, through the death of one of her young children, the death of her husband and, later, of one of her sons in early manhood. She suffered all along from the burden of her mystical experience and from her share in the passion of Christ.

Time and again, she was warned that true values are not found in worldly goods, but in the apparently negative paradox of pain and sacrifice, so contrary to the Greek ideals of the time of Christ, and to almost every tendency of our modern world, more concerned with avoiding discomfort and effort than with sacrificing anything for the common good.

Conchita took as a symbol of her apostolate a large cross, at the center of which was the heart of Jesus, both surmounted by the wings of the Holy Spirit. Another Mexican, Archbishop Martinez, must have been influenced by her, consciously or unconsciously, when he suggested the same symbol in his book, *The Sanctifier*.**

3) *Action of the Holy Spirit*

The all-important effect of the Third Person of the Trinity, the principle of life and love, the Holy Spirit transforming all things from what they are into active participants in the life of God, is stressed again and again with great vividness and power. The so-often forgotten member of the Godhead receives here his full due as the Goodness of all that is good, the Love of all that is loving, the Life of all that is alive. He is shown to be closer to us than our own soul, more intimate to us than we are to ourselves, so deeply involved in our daily thoughts and actions that nothing worthwhile could ever come from us without his inspiration, and

**English tl., St. Anthony Guild Press, Paterson, N.J.

yet his constant whispering leaves us free at all times to choose the way of light or that of darkness.

Until the very end, Conchita led the life of light, the life of the spirit in direct communication with the ineffably Other, who consented, through the incarnation of Christ, to become our brother. They spoke in tender exchanges for over forty years. On the last of her days on earth, on March 3, 1937, it is said that a few moments after she expired, her death-mask fleetingly assumed the countenance of Christ.

VII

LOUISA JAQUES

LOUISA JAQUES
(Sister Mary of the Holy Trinity, Poor Clare of Jerusalem) (1901-1942)

The ways of Providence are varied and often strange in the eyes of men. In some instances, the spiritual evolution of God's chosen children is smooth and continuous, with no other obstacle than the natural imperfection of humanity. In others, everything seems to conspire against spiritual perfection, which is achieved only after many years have elapsed and many obstacles have been overcome. Such is the case of Louisa Jaques who came "home" at the age of thirty-eight and died four years later.

Louisa Jaques was born in 1901 in Pretoria, Transvaal, South Africa, the daughter of French-speaking Swiss Calvinist missionaries. Her mother died in giving birth to her. Her father then took her back to Switzerland with two elder sisters, entrusting her education to an aunt she calls her "Little Mother."

Her health was poor: a serious lung disease left her occasionally spitting blood. One of her sisters married and settled in America, her other relatives remained in Africa. Louisa refused to join them, but stayed alone in Switzerland with her "Little Mother."

There is little in the early childhood of Louisa Jaques that seems to forecast her vocation as a contemplative. Her education by her "Little Mother" had inspired in her a devotional love for her family, father, stepmother and sisters, although the circumstances of their lives kept them apart most of the time. Her religious instruction was elementary. Of the major dogmas of revelation she knew nothing, nor did she believe in the divinity of Christ. All this was to be changed suddenly by an extraordinary apparition.

In the night of February 13/14, 1926, when Louisa — at the age of 25 — had reached a point of deep religious doubt, and while repeating to herself, "There is no God," she had a vision of a nun in brown habit standing near her bed.

"I saw the shadowy form of a woman coming into the room through the casement as through a French window. She approached quickly and noiselessly. There she stood, near the foot of my bed, without touching it. She had wide sleeves, and her hands were crossed inside them. I could not see her face because she seemed to have a sort of cowl on her head, something I had never seen before. She may simply have had her veil lowered. She was tall and straight — out of breath and panting as if she had been running — and from time to time she turned her head toward the window by which she had entered, as though someone were waiting for her outside. . . .

"She frightened me very much. I thought it was death in person who had come for me! It was not a ghost or an illusion. It was a *human being*. I could have touched her. I saw her breathe and turn her head. I was petrified with fear. . . . She must have stayed part of the night, for later when I awoke after having dozed awhile, it seemed to me she was still there.

"I quickly closed my eyes again in order not to see her any more! She said nothing — yet a ray of light had penetrated into my despair. 'Before losing all hope in God, there is still one thing I can do: I will go and pray in a convent.' "

Having no money and no work, Louisa was forced to accept the first opportunity that was offered to her: a position of governess of a small boy in Milan, Italy. While employed as a governess in Milan, Louisa had visited the churches rather than the museums.

"At Santa Maria delle Grazie, the Dominican monastery which possesses Leonardo da Vinci's fresco of the Last Supper, there was to be Benediction of the Blessed Sacrament for a number of days — in a side-chapel where I could see many lights. There was singing and many people were kneeling. I had no idea what was going on, but I was drawn there. The priests seemed to me like maniacs, constantly repeating the same gestures as rapidly as possible. I thought the people were crazy to worship candles. As to what they were saying, I did not even care to know. I was indifferent. When the crowd left, I remained and prayed.''

Beneath the indifference Louisa claims, there must have been some real hunger, for she did remain and prayed. She began going to early Masses. The religion itself meant nothing to her, but something in the churches exercised an irresistible attraction upon her.

Suddenly, she learned that a very capable and well-educated friend, Verena, whose ideas had been like a beacon light to her, had become a Catholic. Verena explained the Eucharist to her:

''He who is so great makes himself very small in order to come to us, hidden under the appearance of bread, so as to help us. . . .If only you knew!''

During that time she had a deep desire to receive Communion. She told a priest in the Cathedral, and he explained she had first to receive instruction. He scribbled a note and said: ''Take this to the Sisters of the Cenacle on the Via Monte di Pietà.'' This was in November, 1927. From then on, Louisa received regular instruction until her baptism on March 18, 1928, which happened to be six days after her ''Little Mother'' died. On March 12, 1928, she returned to Switzerland for the funeral of her ''Little Mother,'' then resumed her job in Milan. She then made her First Communion, which brought no sensible impressions, and she was confirmed several weeks later. On the occasion of a later Communion, she had an unforgettable experience of fire, light and warmth.

Without knowing much about the religious life, she felt a strong call to it and began on her free time from her job as a governess to make the rounds of convents — always without success, since she was obviously in poor health and had no dowry.

Her sister Alice, who was sick in America, sent her a succession of cables begging her to come and help her, but she had firmly decided to enter a convent. Her father and stepmother then announced they were coming to spend a year on vacation in Switzerland. Louisa was torn between love for her family and an ever-stronger religious vocation which painfully hurt her Protestant parents. After different attempts at entering several convents, she was once again refused entry, always because of her poor health. She finally consented to spend some time with her family. Religious differences were reconciled through a mutual effort of charity — then her parents returned to Africa.

In 1931, Louisa was accepted as a postulant in a teaching order, spent two years in a Teachers' College, then took over a class in Neuchatel. Her vows were postponed several times, because of the temptations she was having of joining a different order, the Poor Clares. She was finally allowed to take her first vows in 1935 and continued teaching in Neuchatel. All the time, her health was poor and she was wasting away — her weight down to eighty-eight pounds. She finally obtained permission to join the Poor Clares and entered an extremely strict convent where she quickly became unpopular and was forced to leave, mostly because of her objections to abusive rigidity. This was on April 10, 1937. She found a temporary job helping a working-class family with six children, then spent some restful time taking care of a convalescent boy in Cortina d'Ampezzo in the Italian Tyrol. She again tried to be accepted in a number of convents but was always rejected because of her prior vows, her ill health and her lack of a dowry. Finally, at the end of her rope, with no employment in sight, she wrote to her father asking him if she could come to the Transvaal. After a month with her parents, she went to Johannesburg and made enquiries at the Carmelite convent there. She took up a position as governess with three Jewish families in succession in order to earn the money for her return trip to Europe. Finally, when all her preparations were made for her return to Europe, a letter of acceptance came from the Johannesburg Carmel — but she decided it was too late. On her way back to Switzerland, she planned one more attempt with the Poor Clares: she would visit Mother Amandine, in Our Lady of Sion Convent, *Ecce Homo,* Jerusalem. All she knew was a name and an address. She reserved her passage — with a balance of three pounds sterling for living expenses! At the last minute, she revealed her plans to her father, who was crushed at the thought that she was still trying to enter a Catholic Convent. She arrived in Jerusalem on June 24, 1938 and was received on June 30.

Only at the age of thiry-eight, when she reached Our Lady of Sion convent in Jerusalem, was her vocation fulfilled. She had found her place. From then on, the conversations with the beyond, which had started earlier, became more and more frequent. In spite of the constant demands made upon her by the community work and religious services, she managed to accumulate an astonishing amount of notes in the course of the four last years of her life. Only a few excerpts are given below; the full collection is worth reading with love and care.

There is an astonishing parallel between the message of Louisa and that of Gabrielle Bossis (See Chapter Eight): all the major themes are the same. In fact, this is not surprising: God does not change his mind. His counsels are valid universally. Truth is one.

The main point in Louisa's notes is *God's love for us* — more specifically, the love of Christ, a man like us, yet God infinitely above us; the love of the Savior for the souls he redeemed at the cost of his lifeblood.

Other important points of Louisa's message are:

1) The Savior's insistence on the *need for the total gift of self to his love*.

2) The Lord's insistence on *spiritual charity,* charity in thought, without which exterior charity is soulless and merely a hypocritical mask.

3) The *important role of confessors* in the direction of souls, and the obedience which souls, through the will of

God, owe to them. God also requires priests to be qualified to fulfill their mission toward souls.

4) The Lord's desire regarding the *vow of victim* on the part of generous souls. He himself explains the meaning of this vow: "The vow of victim means to imitate my eucharistic life."

A progression may be seen in Louisa's spirituality coinciding with her entrance into the Poor Clare convent of Jerusalem.

1) The Lord insists first of all, and almost exclusively, on teaching detachment and the stripping of oneself of self-concern.

— Detachment by dispossessing oneself of external things.

— Detachment from oneself rather than from others.

— Stripping oneself of one's own interests rather than of those of others.

2) Then he teaches her the two ways to cooperate with his holy will.

— Passive cooperation: "Let me direct things" (Note 99).

— Active cooperation: "It is sufficient to be" (Notes 210, 282).

3) Finally, he teaches her the value of the hidden life, which he compares to his own.

— Union with God in everything we do.

— The offering, even by a vow, of our life as a holocaust for the glory of God and the good of souls.

These three phases correspond closely with the classical stages of mystical growth: the cleansing (purgative), the illuminative, and the unitive.

Her Autobiography, begun on February 13, 1942, was written by Louisa (Sister Mary of the Holy Trinity) at the explicit request

— almost at the command — of her confessor. It is to him that it is addressed, and it contains the story of her life and of the development of her vocation as summarized above.

The spiritual notes begin with an undated entry, then a few entries dated 1940. All later entries are not dated, but only identified by serial numbers, totalling six hundred and sixty-five, followed by a section in which Sister Mary comments on the Way of the Cross.

The spirit in which Sister Mary was receiving these messages may be judged by the following texts:

33. "Do not be disturbed at repeating to your father [her spiritual director] what I say to you: there is nothing extraordinary in it. I speak to each soul. If there are some who do not hear me, it is because they do not listen to me."

156. "Perhaps they will say you are sentimental in your piety and that you attribute feeble and inadequate utterances to me. Yes, what you retain is incomplete, but you have not attributed too much kindness to me: you have had only a glimpse of a particle of God's ineffable mercy."

271. "You are still astonished that I say only ordinary, quite simple things to you, which everyone knows. I am more simple than you — yes, I the Eternal Wisdom!"

From the very beginning, the notes of Louisa Jaques have the ring of truth. We have here, expressed with clarity and simplicity, the classical program of spiritual perfection, not only for an individual soul, but as a means of salvation for the whole world.

Excerpts from the Notes of Sister Mary of the Holy Trinity (Louisa Jaques)

1. "Forget yourself! Do not concern yourself with your spiritual or material needs. When you have all you need, you deprive me of the joy of taking care of you."

2. "Do not defend yourself; set no value on your rights; let me

have the pleasure of defending you at the right time. Be silent, silent. . . .as I am.''

3. "Make me a present, my little fiancée, of all the unnecessary words you do not speak, of every object that is not indispensable, even if allowed, of all weariness, suffering that others will never guess and that you will hide to prove your love to me, and because I have such need of your gifts.''

8. "I am happy because you have come at last. I await many others like yourself in my Church, in my house. To attract them, do all that I tell you.''

31. "The most important work is not that which you do: it is that which you allow me to do among you.''

37. "Do not worry about the result of your work: it is I who give it growth and fruitfulness in the measure in which it is entrusted to me.''

40. "The more you give me, the more I will increase your capacity for giving.''

42. "Oh, how full I am of compassion! And how I desire — I *need* — the generosity of some to make reparation for others!''

45. "So many anxieties and shadows in your heart! Think of me, of me: perfect Beauty, Splendor, Peace, Life, Truth, Holiness — of me, your God, who loves you!''

55. "Do not be restless; do not be anxious. Everything passes away except your God.''

56. "Do not be afraid of coming to me, do not complain, even to your father [confessor]. If you have certain difficulties in your exterior life, have you not my tenderness for your inner life?

"I see all the sufferings, all the efforts, all the injustices, and I grant the desire of each soul not only with perfect justice, but according to my love which gives in a divine way.''

64. "Happy are the families and convents that have sick members! Because by being visited, the sick safeguard the practice of gentleness and patience. They expiate, they bear my likeness, the image of Christ suffering in the Church.

"A house where there are no sick people runs the risk of living more for itself than for me."

66. "People have a false idea of me: they take me for a master who distributes his favors according to his whims, and who enforces his will. Do you understand that I enforce nothing? I am powerless before your liberty. It is I who beg for your love."

69. "I am crucified through your liberty."

80. "A religious who has not made the vow of victim belongs before all else to her community. And God, though he is the absolute Master of her destiny, takes into account her duties toward her community.

"A religious who has made the vow of victim is entirely delivered up to God's good pleasure, whatever may be her obligations to her community. She is altogether God's."

81. "However poor and useless your life may be, you are responsible for the souls you know — for their lack of faith, and their ignorance of your Jesus. You are responsible in the measure in which you understand."

86. "Yes, there is a multitude of victims who save love and justice from destruction. Those who are passive victims glorify me by their patience in bearing the consequences of sins they have not committed — by their charity which makes reparation and pardons.

"But those who offer themselves voluntarily to make expiation glorify me more: they give the greatest proof of love; they are my sheep who know me and know my voice. Will you do that?"

92. "My enemies are: lying, especially that lack of sincerity which paralyzes so many souls because they will not acknowledge to themselves their most hidden intentions; carelessness and ignorance due to laziness; agitation and disorder; noise: noise of words, noise of selfish desires, the noise that men invent to distract themselves and forget me.

"My friends are: truth, sincerity, silence, order, and that respect which discovers me in all creatures."

102. "There must be victims who mingle their blood with that of Calvary — that is, (victims in the cause of) justice, order, divine wisdom and the demands of sanctity.

"There must be victims who bear witness to my word, in order that it may be passed on as a living thing and that it may be perpetuated accurately.

"Will you be one?"

109. "When suffering is joined to love, the proofs of love given through suffering are a true reparation offered to God. It is giving God something he does not have in his heaven."

111. "I give fullness of joy to the soul who has truly met me and who receives me. She then renounces all secondary things without pain, provided she may keep her God."

113. "Happiness lies in a hidden life. Happiness is to live in the friendship of the Holy Trinity."

116. "This is love: to clothe others with that which will make them pleasing to God.

"To give them even our ideas, the best of our thoughts — not only to tolerate their approbation of them, but to *adorn* them with all that can make them beautiful.

"It was thus that I gave all my blood. I continue to give my body to the human race, to give my spirit, my thoughts . . . the best of my thoughts.

"Do you understand that? God's thoughts are given to man!

"Not only do I give them to him, but I inspire him so gently with them that they become his own, as part of his being. So that he may resemble me and please God. I adorn him with one of the splendors of Christ: his thoughts. That is Love!"

126. "Give without limit, without providing for the future. The future is myself!"

128. "These are two very different things: when you are kind to a soul whom, in the bottom of your heart, you do not esteem; or when you use your kindness to seek and find the beauty hidden in a soul you are not inclined to esteem."

135. "You will be judged by your response to my calls, by the love you will have had for me in all circumstances, on all occasions."

138. "When you have the consolation of creatures, I hide myself and am silent. But when creatures make you suffer, you have my consolation, my support, my intimacy."

139. "You must give with delicacy, you must give invisibly, in my way, so that those who benefit by the gift, not knowing whence it comes, thank God. Then I reward you at once by increasing your love."

140. "Yes, those who seek find, and I give to those who ask of me. But I have the joy of satisfying beyond all expectations the soul who does not express any desire, but awaits me.

"When you ask graces of me for yourself or for others, your capacity for receiving is limited to your request; when you await me, asking for nothing but myself, there is no limit in your heart. As soon as a soul awaits me, I come to her. I have countless ways of approaching and speaking to her. It is love that will make her discover my language."

145. "Do you believe I will abandon you at the moment of death, you who are so wretched you cannot live without me? As a mother embraces her newborn child, so will I enfold you in my love, because you are my tiny child, and I know you cannot do without me."

153. "All that the Father has, he has given me. Nothing is wanting to me but your heart with its free will, which is yours. It is that I ask of you."

165. "If there were more voluntary victims, there would be fewer involuntary victims who are obliged to submit to the terrible consequences of sins they have not committed.

"I desire an army of victims who offer themselves voluntarily to suffer the heavy chastisements the world has brought upon itself by turning away from God.

"These victims know me and unite themselves to me by choosing Calvary in order to follow me.

"But the chastisements that befall the whole universe strike a multitude of souls who are not prepared to suffer injustice and who are in danger of losing their love and faith."

172. "The soul that belongs to me no longer belongs to any particular one, but like me and with me, she belongs to the human race."

191. "Yes, there are many souls who serve me without receiving any consolation from me: their fidelity in that state shows a very great love."

194. "During my life, I spoke in parables so that those who were disposed to understand me might do so."

210. "Beware of keeping up appearances, of seeking to explain yourself, of justifying yourself, of making yourself known, if there has been some mistake. It is enough to be: that alone stands before God, before eternity."

215. "You ask me for graces because you think of my omnipotence. Why do you forget that my action depends upon yours?

"It is with each soul as I said to St. Catherine of Siena, 'Your measure will be my measure.'"

227. "The time you have spent in praying and loving has been the most useful time of your life: then you have obeyed your vocation. All that is done apart from me, apart from Love, is wasted."

237. "Wherein lies the limit of my power over you? In your confidence."

238. "Your first duty now is to hold yourself ready and to listen to me."

243. "You have never seen me, but you hear me. My voice is so hidden in the depths of your being that it seems to you as if it were you who are speaking. I am so immersed in you that I agree to become you in order to win you entirely. But I am also outside you.

"It is when I am silent that you feel the void, that you feel you cannot replace me, that you have proof it is I, JESUS the Savior, who speak to you.''

247. ''I wish every soul would understand she has a motive for living greater than herself: to take part in the establishment of my kingdom — and that her taking her part is necessary to me in order that my creation may achieve the fullness of its destiny.''

248. ''In order to receive the gift of faith, you must remember you are creatures dependent upon one another. As your physical life is dependent upon the help of your brothers, so is your spiritual life.''

''Your mind must open itself to other minds in order to communicate with them, and also in order to receive the words of those who are my servants, above all my priests, who pass on my doctrines, who speak as my other selves.

''Independent free-will opposes itself unconsciously to my grace, whereas the willing submission of your thoughts and souls irresistibly attracts it.''

''The Holy Spirit breathes where he will. When you endeavor to detain him or bind him by the limits of your understanding, he escapes. But he never refuses to give himself to those who appeal to him.

''I do not strive against your free-will: I silently offer myself with my bloody and luminous cross, and with my Beatitudes.

''If I am repulsed, I wait until I am truly welcome — and I send my servants to plead my cause. Ah, how I need your human cooperation!

''The Communion of Saints, fellowship, brotherly mutual help are gifts of God, the human means given to you: use them!

''Instead of developing your talents, seek rather to welcome God's gifts: your souls will be loaded with imperishable riches!''

249. ''The inner effort is what matters: it *is* for eternity. The visible result matters little.''

250. ''Your life has been calmed and enlightened. So will it be with every soul if she desires it, if she is attentive.''

254. "Living the truth means vigilance and courage; it means exposing oneself to humiliation, abandonment, contempt — but it also means handing on my *living* doctrine, communicating it by example."

261. "I cannot dwell in a soul that judges others."

274. "Souls brilliant with natural talents have disappointed me more often than little people. Do you believe it? It is my joy to make myself little with the little ones."

281. "At death, before God and for eternity, this alone will remain in your being: your love.

"And in the hands of God, wherewith you weave your crown, there will be found nothing but what you have given him."

282. "There are many things that you might tell your sisters and that I wish you would communicate to them. But I wish you to speak to them through your silence: that will be your way of passing on my messages: it is enough to *be*."

284. "In the secret intimacy of the soul, I speak softly, for a soul must come to me *of herself*."

293. "I do not hide myself, I am very near you, within you. I am very simple. You seek me too far away, as an inaccessible God. I am a God who has made himself your Brother.

"Because you seek me too far off, you pass beside me without seeing me, and you no longer feel the infinite sweetness my presence brings in your soul."

299. "Faith is also a form of obedience: the submission of the mind."

305. "I wait: long have I waited for you — for other souls, still longer. Centuries may pass, but I do not tire of waiting for that voluntary impulse of souls who come closer to me. Ever since I was 'lifted up from the earth,' I draw them all to myself."

308. "I am the Source from which the waters flow inexhaustibly, with abundance — but you must *come* to the source to drink. Come, all of you! Do not stop by the way! Life eternal is near you: accept it!"

312. "Gentleness, patience, joy!

"Gentleness, patience, joy!

"Gentleness, patience, joy!

"Give me these three things in your external life, in your judgments, your thoughts, your feelings.

"Gentleness is the fruit of love; patience is the fruit of faith; joy is the fruit of hope.

"When these alone fill your heart, then I will reign in it as King!"

319. "If you only knew what a great thing it is to appear before God! If the soul is ready, why wish to detain her? Think more of her than of yourselves."

327. "When you do not think of yourself, my grace visits you, and I provide what is necessary for you; when you act on your own, I leave you to your own care."

328. "You say little children have no great merit since they have no great struggles. The value of your life does not lie in any personal merit brought about by your generosity. It will lie in using your generosity to let me live in you. Do you understand?"

355. "Just as I am near you, so is beauty near you, even when the most extreme poverty reigns.

"Have you not noticed that when everything is in its place according to order and harmony, when there is silence and peace between objects, and cleanliness, have you not noticed how my life envelops things with grace and beauty? Yes, objects share in the harmony of the universe when you respect them and dispose of them with care.

"Beauty is near you if you will welcome it into your house and give it attention."

364. "Why do you fear death? Do you doubt me? For your sins, see: here is my Mercy! For your cares, your anxieties, your desires, here is my Providence! For your weaknesses, here is my Omnipotence! It is my joy to give you hour by hour sufficient strength, to have you entirely dependent upon my love."

366. "I ask four things of the souls who bind themselves more closely to me by the vow of victim:

"That they listen to me more than speak to me.

"That they strive to reproduce my deeds, my way of acting rather than my words.

"That they stand before men as they stand before God, in a state of poverty that begs rather than in a state of spiritual wealth that gives alms of its superfluity. Poor souls without pretension are in the truth. And because they *are true,* they do not hurt their fellow-creatures, and my grace can work with them.

"That they confine their efforts to spreading my Spirit, my gentleness and my kindness which does not dwell on evil, but overcomes evil with good. By being exacting with no one but themselves, they will help souls through silence and respect to receive the graces their fidelity and sacrifices will obtain from God."

372. "There are souls who reject my words, who do not believe in my divinity, and yet act toward their neighbor as I did. They have given me their lives, but they have not given me their hearts; their hearts remain closed to joy. That is why my mercy sometimes grants them sufferings to save them from the narrow boundaries of their contentment."

376. "Do not be surprised if I invite those who are mine to let themselves be destroyed by love!"

385. "Now, when receiving me each morning in Holy Communion, it is you who absorb me; at your death, it is I who will absorb you, to unite you to myself. Who do you fear? Prepare yourself!"

395. "I am more human than you!"

407. "Sanctity is allowing me to live in you; it is giving me your human nature so that I may live on among you.

"It is simple: children understand it!"

414. "Remember that, like yourself, your sisters need to feel

loved. It is a necessity, because you are creatures in the state of evolution, and you *need* the love of others in order to develop.''

488. ''It is not on account of your qualities that I love you, nor on account of your virtues — if you had any. If you had any virtue, you would owe it to me. Your own part would consist merely in having received my gift.

''It is not because of your defects or sins that I love you: it is because I have given you life, and because I continue to give it to you each day; and it is because I have redeemed you at the price of much suffering. Because I am Love, all Love, I cannot cease communicating to my creatures the joy of loving, the joy of sharing my happiness.''

507. ''I always accomplish that which I have decided to do. I use the human elements that your free actions determine. Therein lie your cooperation and your responsibility.

''You provide me with means that favor the accomplishment of my will; you also provide me with other means that oppose my will and delay its accomplishment. But my will triumphs through all human circumstances: it has its hour.''

529. ''Yes, I ask for an army of victims scattered everywhere — for everywhere evil is mingled with good: in the organization of states as in that of communities, in families as in each soul.''

550. ''You are in God, in his power, as leaves abandoned to a breath of wind. And I have made myself depend upon you! I, your God, dependent, that I may dwell on your altars in the Real Presence, dependent so as to give you my life through Holy Communion, dependent so as to give you my grace through the sacraments, dependent so that I can enter your heart and reign there.

''Do you understand?''

578. ''There are so many misconceptions and misunderstandings among souls of good will because you create for yourselves a too limited, a too narrow idea of God. The perfections of God do not exclude each other.

"Why do you wish to imprison God and what he asks within the limits of your own ideal which varies according to place and time? What the Church tells you about God is sufficient to disperse all misunderstandings. Why are you not content with what the Church says? 'He who is not against me is with me.'

"God is life, and wherever life circulates, he shows something of his power, goodness and magnificence.

"In my Father's house, there are many mansions."

595. "I wish people to be able to say at your death, 'She was a saint: she did very well all she did.' That perfection in the common life is the sanctity I ask of you, nothing else. And in that work, you will have more than my help; it is I who will do it in you. I desire it of you and of each one of your sisters."

600. "When your soul is at peace, you believe I am pleased with you. When it is troubled by great storms, do not believe I am not pleased with you. You do not *feel* it, but it is in those moments I come to your help and draw you closer to me."

606. "Go down into the depths, into the innermost depths of yourself: you will find me there.

"Make silence reign in the innermost depths of your being: you will hear my voice.

"Listen to me, do what I tell you: I will transform you!"

610. "I command the elements with power: my voice pierces them; my will imprints itself upon them.

"I do not command souls: I ask them, because I have created them free."

611. "My little daughter, you belong to the Holy Trinity.

"The Father created you to give you the Son, who redeemed you to give you the Father and the Holy Spirit who transforms your soul."

622. "Some call the way that leads to my heart 'love,' others call it 'suffering.' Love without suffering does not lead to my heart: love and suffering are inseparable — inseparable in their growth, inseparable in their demands, indissolubly united. But there is a

fruit they infallibly produce and which men often forget to name when they speak of the way that leads to me. I will tell it to you, my little daughter: it is *joy*. Keep in your heart this threefold name of the way that leads to my heart:

"Love-suffering-joy."

633. "The soul who honors me most is not the one who has suffered most. It is the one who has most perfectly transformed all her sufferings into love and joy. Yes, all her sufferings, even the smallest annoyance and little disappointments. Her love glorifies me already on earth."

636. "My little daughter, you never present yourself alone before God: in your soul, there is the Holy Trinity — and there is also a tiny portion of the whole Church.

"You are a link in that infinite chain, having received graces merited by those who came before you. And a great number of other links will join it later. You are in interdependent fellowship with one another, and that for eternity."

650. "There are several forms of humility: that which admits your nothingness, your unworthiness, speaks according to wisdom and truth. But it is also a form of humility not to speak of yourself because you do not think of yourself: you think only of me.

"I love that silence concerning yourself."

VIII

GABRIELLE BOSSIS

GABRIELLE BOSSIS
(1874-1950)

The ways of mystical perfection are not limited to those who have
made religious vows: God's favors are lavished on whomsoever he
pleases, sometimes most surprisingly. Here, for instance, is an
elegant, refined woman of the world whose whole life was linked
with an activity that many churchmen had scorned as sinful: the
theater. Perhaps the choice of this favorite daughter was made
precisely to offset any clerical prejudice and to demonstrate that
existential contact with God is open to those called to it, whatever
their profession.

Gabrielle Bossis was born in Nantes, France, in 1874, the
youngest of four children in a wealthy middle-class family.

From an extremely shy, fearful and tearful little girl, more
often found by herself in corners than playing with other children,
she grew up into a graceful, joyous, high-spirited young girl, very
sociably inclined, although possessed of a secret yearning for God
and the things of the spirit which led to frequent contemplation.

Because of her father's wealth, there was no need for Gabrielle
to earn her living. Her early years passed peacefully in her home in
Nantes, or at the family summer residence in Fresne on the Loire
river. Yet she was always very active. She obtained a degree in
nursing, assisted in various parish projects, embroidered church
vestments for the missions and practiced the fine arts open to a
young lady of her rank: music, painting and sculpture, while still
finding time for her favorite sport, horseback riding, and attending
many dancing parties and social gatherings.

Quite late in life, she discovered that she had another talent: that of writing the kind of entertaining and thoroughly moral comedies so much in demand by church clubs, a task ''not so easy as one imagines,'' as Daniel-Rops commented.

Her first play, written for a club in Anjou, in which she acted the principal part, was such a success that before long her name became known throughout France and even in far distant countries. From this time on, until two years before her death, she traveled extensively, producing her own plays and continuing to act in the principal role. Those who remember her still remark on the extraordinary youthfulness of her mind and body, the golden hair that resisted the touch of time, the ringing laughter, the unfailing charm of the successful playwright and actress.

At the age of sixty-two, while traveling to Canada on the ''Ile de France,'' a dialogue with an inner Voice began for good, continuing until two weeks before her death.

Although no records remain of further travels, we can still trace her wandering footsteps by the colorful place names mentioned in her journals: Carthage, Tunis, Algiers, Constantine, and many towns in France, Italy and other parts of Europe.

Gabrielle Bossis never married. Until the illness that carried her off, her health was impeccable. Yet when death came, she welcomed it as she had welcomed life — with the same high-hearted love and joy. ''My heart is getting weaker every day,'' she wrote on May 9, 1950. ''I have taken neither food nor liquid for three days. So I shall be leaving soon. Rejoice with me. *Magnificat* . . . and there will be no more partings.'' She died on June 9, 1950.

Besides her natural joyfulness, Gabrielle Bossis had revealed since early childhood a serious attraction to spiritual matters. When the hidden treasure of her unusual inner life came to the notice of the Franciscan priest who was directing her, he felt convinced she had a vocation for convent life and brought pressure upon her to become a nun. Gabrielle resisted his suggestion with great determination, feeling led by an interior guide and by the supreme attraction of a love surpassing all human loves that led to her refusal of the many proposals of marriage that came to her.

On very rare occasions in her early life, Gabrielle had been surprised by a mysterious voice which she believed — though not without occasional anxious questioning — to be that of Christ. In the course of years, her doubts were progressively resolved. The objectivity of the voice and the reality of God behind it were clearly confirmed. At the same time, a reason was given as to why a veil must remain, as to why she could not see God face to face: God was hiding intentionally behind a curtain. He was offering her a merry chase so that she might pursue him with greater ardor and merit. Yet the veil was thin and, though unseen, God was always there.

Her dialogue with the Lord — which constitutes the essence of her notes — began in earnest in 1936 on her trip to Canada. From then on, all doubts were dismissed. Gabrielle fully accepted the fact of her communication with the Lord and managed to live successfully her double life: as a much acclaimed and beloved woman of the world, and as the secret bride of Christ.

Perhaps the most astonishing aspect of Gabrielle's spirituality was the simple, natural, joyful ease with which she entered the secret garden of God's love. She seems to have been spared all the torturing preludes, the ways of purgation and illumination, the dark nights of the senses and of the spirit that always seemed to be the only avenues to contemplative perfection. None of this is found in her writings. She seems to glide into supernatural states with the ease of a fish swimming in the waters for which it was made, or of a child playing with the toys she had always known were hers. Her spirituality is one of simplicity and joy, true childlikeness, and an astonishing harmonization of worldly values with those of God. She did not have to renounce her theatrical vocation. To the end she was always coquettishly dressed, adulated, fêted; she traveled with ease and lived on a level of luxury. Apparently, she never had to renounce anything other than the joys of marriage and motherhood. Yet her inner spirit was so pure that she managed to ride the waves of worldly success without ever drowning out the voice of her true Lover.

Besides the extraordinary example Gabrielle Bossis managed to give on how to successfully lead a twofold life — temporal and spiritual — she also left us in her diary, *He and I,* a rich legacy of thoughts and counsels received in the course of her conversations with the Lord. Once, when Gabrielle was marvelling how quickly the first French edition of her diary (*Lui et moi*) had sold out, Jesus said to her: "Do you know what you are doing in writing these pages? We're removing the false idea that this intimate life of the soul is possible only for the religious in the cloister. In reality, my secret and tender love is for every human being living in this world. There is not one that does not have a mysterious yearning for it. And how true it is that each one wants to see someone live my love so that he or she may discover the means of reaching me."

Her conversations with the Lord may perhaps be grouped under six headings: (1) The Hidden God, (2) God's Hunger for Love: His Self-Revelation, (3) How to Love God: Our Response, (4) Freedom, Providence and Destiny, (5) The Call of Perfection: Love of Neighbor, and (6) Death: The Final Act of Love.

1) The Hidden God

From the very beginning of her supernatural experiences, Gabrielle wondered about the origin of the mysterious Voice. She was not sure whether it came from outside or from her own imagination. Confirmation regarding the authenticity of the messages she is receiving and the necessity of loving the unseen, hidden God is given to her repeatedly.

January 17, 1940 — "You don't always perceive me in the same manner, but don't let darkness stop you from moving forward. Humble yourself and keep going on your way with faith. You may not see me or feel me, yet I am there: Love itself, holding out my arms to you. Nothing ever makes me lose sight of my children on earth. Their ideas and their thoughts never last long, and so they imagine mine are the same. But I am perfect Constancy, the same yesterday, today and forever. I am the Presence, the loving Glance. The whole universe is cradled in me. I am this very moment of time, and I am eternity. I am the lavishness of Love, the One who calls, so that you may come without fear and throw yourself upon my heart.''

January 26, 1940 — ''Don't you understand that the bonds of my union with a soul must be tightened as it draws near to eternity? Try to be no longer in yourself, but in me. You were touched when you read that I was in the gospels, hidden in the sacrament of the words. But how much more am I present in the sacrament of man himself. O my children who live in grace, let us never abandon one another!''

June 20, 1941 — ''Believe without trying to define.''

April 23, 1942 — ''You may not feel me beside you at all times, yet I am always there. Sometimes I come closer, as I did yesterday in the garden when you said, 'Good morning, my darling God!' It seemed almost as if I had answered you. I hide behind a veil, so that you may learn to walk by faith, and merit through learning. My love surprises you: there is only one explanation — God's extravagance. The only thing you need to do is to believe with utter simplicity in this love of an all-powerful Being, a Being totally different from you, and surrender to his infinitely delicate and tender might. Become a captive of Love and pray for grace; love me with my Love and trust in full.''

July 15, 1943 — ''Very little keeps you from seeing me.''

November 23, 1944 — ''I am like a master teaching from behind a curtain so as to hide his great love for his pupils; a player of games who eludes pursuers so as to enliven and lengthen the chase.''

February 20, 1945 — ''Don't get the notion that you are talking with a memory, a past idea, a remote God: you are talking to me, fully alive in you, to your ever-present Presence.''

April 26, 1948 — "On earth, you always have to guess. I'm always hidden behind the door."

October 20, 1949 — "A man will leave everything — every material thing — to follow God alone, the One he loves without having seen him. This, my child, is the whole secret of the delight a soul can give its God."

November 10, 1949 — "Establish strongly in your mind the notion that this, my Presence in you, is neither allegory, fantasy nor metaphor. It is not some tale you are hearing, nor an event experienced by someone else. It has to do with you and me, it has to do with a reality to be lived."

2) God's Hunger for Love: His Self-Revelation

The contrast is striking between the God of wrath and terror of the Old Testament and this Mendicant of Love, the tender, suffering and human Christ who begs us to share his agony, who showers gifts upon us and is wounded by our indifference. In few mystical writers do we find expressions of such simple intimacy as when Gabrielle speaks to her "Darling God" and Christ explains God's need for tenderness. The very humanity of the conversation elevates it to the level of the divine.

Volumes of theology could be written on such pregnant thoughts as the following: "My little girl, continue me." — "Don't leave me!" — "I am alone to defend myself." — "Adore my hunger-love for you." — "Try to be for me a little of what I am for you."

God is hiding for our own good. He is hungering for our love. How are we to respond to this inner appeal?

June 26, 1937 — "Is it because I am God that you believe I have no need of tenderness?"

September 19, 1940 — "It's a strange thing, isn't it, that a creature can comfort its God. And yet this is a fact. My love reverses the roles, inventing new ways for people to reach me — by allowing them to give me a protective tenderness. So great is my need of all your ways of loving, all your ways of being tender!''

October 11, 1940 — ''Don't ask that I be loved: offer every one of your deeds for this purpose. Nothing could be more soothing for me. Strange as it may seem to you, there is a kind of grace I cannot give unless you ask me for it. Such grace is the work of two parties: your Christ and man himself. You know how much I love to be one with you: we each have our own part to play — and since I never impose upon you, your part is to call upon me. You must make me act in your company: thus do I live my life again on earth.

''That is why I sometimes ask you, 'My little girl, continue me.' Your life is a gift from me: give it back to me through all your deeds. Don't be overwhelmed by this great task of making God live: it is so simple, if you only knew!

''Imagine what would happen if at this moment all the people on earth let me live in them through grace! What a sight for heaven — for indeed all of you are performing before the angels and saints. You see, you are still on stage. . . .

''If only you thought of all this, wouldn't you strive for greater perfection in everything you do? And if you remembered I never lose sight of you — as indeed I do not — wouldn't you be more careful, wouldn't you love me a little more?

''My poor little ones, don't miss anything that could increase your tenderness: such oversight is the only source of your unhappiness. Whenever you come upon some moving truth or thought, keep it in your mind the whole day long, and look at it as if you were seeing me in a mirror.

''Call to me often: isn't an earthly father happy when he hears his little one's appeals? Sometimes he does not answer immediately in the hope that the child will call again. Do you remember when I seemed to rebuke the Canaanite woman? I wanted to lead her to her so beautiful and humble answer. . . .And so, if I seem not to hear you, call again and you will give me joy.

''I am always eagerly awaiting you — particularly my little

ones, my very poor ones. The weakest are already right within my
heart. Oh, happy are the underprivileged!''

November 9, 1940 — ''Be assured human nature is unable to
love suffering as such. But supernature uses suffering as a means to
serve God, either for his sake — and this is the more perfect — or
for the sake of some grace we wish to obtain, if such is the Father's
will.

''My little children, always be one with me in my pain. In order
to quicken your will to love, you may want to choose some
particular sufferings: those of my childhood, my adolescence or
my public life; those inflicted by people's words and deeds, or by
the ingratitude of those I loved; the sorrows imposed on my mother
and friends at the time of my passion.

''Don't waste a single one of your precious sufferings: steep
them in supernatural joy.''

January 9, 1941 — ''Come and watch me suffer in the garden,
as if you had been there on that very night: for it is now that same
night, since God sees all time at a glance. Don't leave me! I am like
a terrified child begging not to be left alone. Stay here, let me know
you are with me: a presence is soothing. Hold my hand: I am only a
poor man full of distress — even though I am God! No one will ever
understand the depth of my desolation. I feel the need of being
surrounded by all my beloved ones, for I see all the powers of evil
let loose, and I am alone to defend myself. Pray with me. Is your
faith in my love any stronger, now that you have seen how deep is
my pain? Give me this token of kindness, this offering of faith!''

May 1, 1941 — ''O my dear children, Love unloved! How
deep this wound I bear! Give comfort, help, repose to love. Poor as
you may be, give everything to love. Lean on my heart, and the
weight of you shall be my joy: I will flow into you as the sap of the
vine flows from root to branches — and you will be my life. You
are nothing at all by yourself, my poor little girl!''

March 20, 1947 — ''Adore my love, my hunger-love for you.
Adore the supremely delicate manner in which I share my secret

thoughts with you and reveal my desires to you. Try to be for me a little of what I am for you. Do you see how difficult it is for me to ask? Your freedom often prevents me from saying what I would like to say to you — as if I had been waiting for you to discover my heart's desires on your own. How great is my joy when you do!''

February 12, 1948 — ''Sometimes I offer gifts in silence. I often think, 'They will understand.' Alas, how many take the gift without paying any attention to the Giver! It is not my honor that suffers, but my love. You, my children who know better, never make Love suffer!''

March 17, 1948 — ''I am thirsty. I have only what people give me: I take nothing.''

October 27, 1948 — ''I have another temple: your soul in the state of grace — a state of I-in-you, since grace is your Christ.''

3) How to Love God: Our Response

Time and again, the same message is given: God is always there, always giving, always loving. But he cannot impose his gifts upon us. It is up to us to open to him and to ask, repeatedly and perseveringly, with growing ardor and hunger. Then only will we receive his gifts and enjoy them in full. The perfect relationship with God is not one of grim submission or dutiful prayer, but a joyful game, a playful exchange of pleasure beyond the paradox of the cross.

Joy and simplicity are the keynote of Gabrielle's message. Our response to God's love should manifest these same qualities. Such a doctrine is a far cry from any gloomy spirituality of mortification and penance. Of course there is room for penance as a form of atonement, but the true Christian climate is one of joy — and there is as much merit in offering God our pleasures as in offering him our pains.

February 14, 1937 — ''In your soul there is a door that leads to the contemplation of God — but you must open it.''

April 7, 1938 — ''From now on, spend your life delighting me:

you will feel transformed. Please me, live for me: this is the true meaning of your divinity.''

April 28, 1939 — ''Enjoy me, give yourself a rest from saying prayers, so that you may delight in my love.''

June 1, 1939 — ''Write! I don't want people to be afraid of me any more: they should see my heart full of love and speak with me as with a dearly beloved brother.

''Some people do not know me at all. For others, I am a stranger, a severe master, a prosecutor. Few come to me as to a member of a beloved family. All the while, my love is there, awaiting them. Tell them to come, to enter, to surrender themselves to love just as they are: I will restore and transform them, and they will know a joy such as they never had before. I alone can give that joy. If only they would come! Tell them to come!''

August 22, 1940 — ''Take power from the power of the saints, from the power of the holy ones: be one with them. Give me the joy of helping and changing you; surrender everything; let yourself go. Tell me often about your deepest longing. Do you imagine I would resist you? You would not know me well if you did. If you are generous, how much more am I! You know the violent storm, the bird of prey? I too carry off: I am the Ravisher. Don't struggle — and because you let yourself be caught, I will bring you into my secret garden among the flowers and the fruit. You will wear the wedding ring on your finger, your step will be in time with mine, and I will stoop down to your littleness so that we may walk together at ease.''

August 29, 1940 — ''My little children, consider my simplicity and how easy it is for you to please me: merely do everything as well as you can for the sake of my love, so as to grow, to proceed, to ascend. Hold out your two weak arms to me: I will help you. We will do the work together, bearing unequal burdens. It is for the father to shoulder the heavier end of things. As long as the small child gazes fondly into the father's eyes, the painful task will not seem so bad. A look of love! What power for you, what joy for me!''

September 12, 1940 — ''Never drain your cup of pleasure to the last drop: keep a little for me, as a sacrifice, my share — do you understand what I mean? — since we are together secretly in all things. If you took it all, what would be left for me? You would be alone with yourself.''

September 14, 1940 — ''Live in my heart. You have discovered the warm nest of the golden-crested wren hidden in your locust tree? It is within reach of any hand — but invisible.

''Call upon the angels to help you climb. So intense is my longing to have you come near, so much do I have to tell you, so much to give you! Come closer, ever-closer.''

January 3, 1943 — ''Why should my people offer me nothing but their trials? Don't you believe your joys would please me just as much — that is, if you give them with proportionate love, your smallest joys with the greatest love?''

April 20, 1945 — ''Then remember the value of a free gift, the gift of self, when offered out of tenderness. What inexpressible joy will be his who receives it! He will multiply his blessings so that the recipient will be lost in wonder and gratitude: 'What have I done to deserve the kindness of my God?' he will ask. And I shall reply, 'You loved him with all your might, and you let him love you.' ''

June 21, 1947 — ''If you offered me your joys and your moments of recreation, I would send you few trials, for it is only your union with me that I am seeking, and as a rule, you come to me only when you are unhappy. Then come — oh, come always!''

September 9, 1948 — ''I am all simplicity: love me simply. When you think of me, and are sorry not to be able to do better, you are loving me. When you do what you must rather than what you would like, you are loving me. When you underestimate yourself and belittle yourself, you are loving me. When you want to pray and regret your wandering thoughts, you are loving me. When you seek in vain for words to express your hunger, you are loving me. When you forgive a cutting remark, or give pleasure for the sake of giving pleasure; when you forget yourself in order to reach me; when you try to surrender everything as if it were the day of your death; when in thought you join the angels and the saints as if you had arrived before your time; and when in the evening you look forward to the morrow that will make us one: you are loving me!"

Now that Gabrielle has considered God's love and man's reaction to it, let us see how she considers three aspects of the God/man relationship.

4) Freedom, Providence and Destiny

We have seen the delicacy with which God is begging for man's response of love. The main reason is that love has value only as a free gift: it cannot be forced upon anyone. The destiny for which we were born is union with God, obtained through our free gift of love. But the only occasion we have to achieve our proper end is this present life: for our freedom will end at the moment of death.

Peace of mind and holiness belong to those who abandon themselves to God's providence. But this abandonment must be an active participation in his will. How this is done is the subject of a further series of revelations excerpted from Gabrielle's diary, concerned with the perfection of moral life.

May 8, 1937 — "Do not go to so much trouble making plans: I am the One who does your thinking for you."

October 4, 1938 — "Above all, trust! When you are anguished and can do nothing about it, just think, 'He will straighten it out for me,' and go back to the peace within me."

August 29, 1940 — "The Holy Trinity resides within each one of you, more or less according to the space you allow him — for as you know, God never forces anyone: He only asks and waits. When you remain faithful, you are assured of the joy — I was going to say of the celestial joy — that heaven receives. Keep this thought before you always: It is while you are living on earth that I enjoy you, my beloved faithful ones. In heaven, it will be you who enjoy me."

November 4, 1940 — "Do you believe at last with all your heart that I created you for the sake of your eternal happiness? I made you out of pure love — not in my interest, but in yours: to give you infinite delight."

March 1, 1945 — "How much comfort people would find and what happiness even in the midst of trials if they only believed that every event in their lives comes from my desire to do them good, and that everything is fitted to the measure of each one."

January 3, 1946 — "You always believe these things just happen. Nothing just happens: I am in everything — and I am all Love."

April 11, 1946 — "Hunt for me everywhere: I will let myself be caught with such joy! How did you expect to find me if you didn't search? As soon as you have found me, give me to others: there are people I am waiting to reach only through you. This is the mission foreseen for you from all eternity. Don't be unfaithful: I was faithful even to the point of torment, of public disgrace."

May 30, 1946 — "When you love me perfectly, more than anything else, all reality, all ideas, everything will be fulfilled in you, because you will have attained the end for which I created and redeemed you."

December 11, 1947 — "Now do you understand a little better the reason why you were born? To be one with me."

January 22, 1948 — "I am like a shy person: I prefer you to discover my love on your own, for I am afraid of speaking about it, lest I seem to be forcing it upon you. There again, you are free. But how great is my joy when of your own free will you seek ways of multiplying our meetings and deepening our intimacy! I let you be the one to come, to call, hiding myself in order to increase your desire for me. And at the moment you believe you are lost, there I come with all my gifts!''

April 26, 1948 — ''How could I not want your entire being when I know you are free?''

February 2, 1949 — ''Rejoice in knowing nothing about the future if only for the chance of abandoning it to me.''

March 30, 1949 — ''My child, consider more often the value of the present, the danger of going back over the past, and the uselessness of gazing into the future. Live the simple moment you hold in your hands, plainly and lovingly.''

April 28, 1949 — ''Your free will with all its opportunities will no longer exist in heaven.''

5) The Call to Perfection: Love of Neighbor

The theme here is our relationship with others. Christ is no longer with us in the flesh. But our neighbor is! What we must do is look upon him as Christ did, and see Christ in him, even through the veil of human degradation and sin. ''The fat lady is Christ'' as Salinger wrote of a drunken old woman. The beauty of a young girl is also Christ. This vocation of seeing Christ is open to all. It is also the way to perfection.

February 14, 1937 — ''You saw my love in the face of that young girl? Be like her always. If my followers were kind to each other, the face of the world would be changed.''

April 9, 1937 — ''You must aim at perfection, but the perfection of your own nature. That is the way to please me.''

June 25, 1937 — ''Do not see sin in mere natural weaknesses: what makes me suffer is indifference.''

January 4, 1938 — ''Consolations? Give them to others!''

January 8, 1939 — ''Do not be vain in any way. What does it matter to you what people think of you? Be happy with the thought that I know you.''

June 1, 1939 — ''Be crucified with me. Being crucified is

being stretched against your nature, against your desires, against the love of self, in poverty, obscurity and obedience to the Father.''

April 9, 1940 — ''Do not believe a saint must look saintly in the eyes of men. He has an outer nature, but his inner nature is the important thing. Some fruit have a rough, even thorny skin that gives no inkling of their sweet and juicy taste. It is the same with my saints: their value is inside their hearts.''

July 25, 1940 — ''Be as gracious toward the little ones as toward the great ones of this world; make a particular effort when you happen to be with people who seem vulgar to you; go to each one with the same gentleness: you are all brothers in me. Was I not everyone's brother? Do not take your eyes off your model.''

September 12, 1940 — ''I start my life on earth all over again with each one of you — my life wedded to yours — if only you choose to invite me. Do you remember how I walked with the disciples at Emmaus? I am doing the same for you, I am walking along the same path with you, the path I chose for you from all eternity — in this family, in this country where you live. It is I who placed you here with a special love. So live here, full of faith, remembering this is where you will gain your heaven, where you will gain eternal love in exchange for this brief moment in time. Pass, then, through this life with an intense desire to answer my tenderness, and with constant eagerness to know me at last — to know me, your loving Savior. You have always been a thought in my eternal mind: it would be only fair for yours to be filled with me, my poor little children so often ungrateful!''

November 12, 1942 — ''My little girl, be assured of this: while I am no longer on earth, your neighbor *is* there.''

October 3, 1944 — ''Be my voice for others. It is not enough to be good: you must be my goodness. Do you see the difference? It is the whole difference between you and me. Forget that you are you: be your Christ, the one who loves you always.''

November 22, 1945 — ''I love to live my life on earth anew through my children. If only you knew how few allow me to do it!''

November 27, 1947 — ''My little girl, do you know when you are speaking like me? When you put kindness and charm in your words, when you touch hearts, when you counter an acid remark with a gracious answer, when you make excuses for someone, when you serve, when you give, when you calm someone who is angry, when you comfort, when you keep an even temper under all circumstances, when you remain humble without seeking to shine, when you are grateful for the kindness of others, when you are generous.''

December 21, 1947 — ''Try to see me more clearly in those around you and your entire relationship with them will be changed.''

November 11, 1948 — ''Practice being more attractive for love's sake. You could do immense good with an affectionate look and a smile. If you keep yourself to yourself, you will remain your own slave.''

May 21, 1942 — ''Would I ask every soul to be holy if this were impossible?''

March 6, 1947 — ''I need every one of you as if you were the only person in the world, as if the universe had been created for you alone — and my love is greater than the universe.''

June 15, 1947 — ''I have called you to union. My invitation is to every man, woman and child. Yet few have heeded it.''

The way of perfection is through a Christ-like life, followed by a holy death. Gabrielle, in her lively joy, speaks well of death.

6) Death: The Final Act of Love

Gabrielle Bossis was more concerned with life than with death — but death was present in her mind as the door to final happiness. Many times in her diary she refers to it in eloquent terms that may serve as a fitting conclusion to the study of her message.

February 26, 1941 — ''Remember this: as one lives, so one dies. If, during this present interval before death, your heart is full of me; if zeal for my kingdom is burning in it; if you thirst for my glory: death will find you in that same state, and you will pass on with a pining of love.

"Passing on: it is no long journey, but merely moving out of earthly life into the other life. This is your true birthday, this is being born to life everlasting. I AM THE LIFE, I, your Christ!"

October 8, 1942 — "Come to me little by little, your heart aflame at the moment of death. And find a sweeter name for death: call it 'the Meeting' — and even now, with only a glimpse of me in the twilight of time, you will stretch out your arms to me."

April 4, 1946 — "Don't be afraid of anything. Death? Of course not! You will receive the grace of clothing yourself in death; you will enter into it as you would enter a task received from me, I helping you see as always."

March 20, 1947 — "You are worried about the passage from this life into the next? But since it is the greatest proof of love you can give me, be glad. Offer your death to me now with complete detachment, ready even for heroism. Say, 'Even if I didn't have to suffer death, I would choose it in order to be more closely united with him.' And in this way you will give me the greatest glory a creature can give its Creator. O precious death of the saints that echoes even in the heavenly courts of the Father's home!

"So don't be afraid of losing your brief life on earth in exchange for the eternal meeting with the Beloved. And since I will be there with you, what a moment of faith, hope and love!"

Final Entries:

May 23, 1950 — Communion of the Sick.

"Poor little soul, you've waited to the very last minute of your life to believe in my boundless compassion, in final forgiveness! Have no more fear of anything. It would wound me if you were afraid. Surrender your whole being to Love, my beloved!"

May 24, 1950 — No more strength. I can scarcely see. I'm scarcely able to love you.

"Take my eyes. Take my voice. Take my love!"

May 25, 1950 — Have I come to the end of my life? Is this the moment when I celebrate my first and last Mass? Where are you, loving Presence? . . . And afterwards, what will it be?

"It will be I; it will be I — FOREVERMORE!"

With the joyful assurance of coming into the presence of Christ, Gabrielle died on June 9, 1950. May she rest in peace with her Lover and Lord.

AFTERWORD

We have now traveled in time and space in the company of remarkable women, each very different from the other, yet all united in the precious gift of their existential contact with the Living God. Inexhaustible lessons may be drawn from their writings, for as soon as we touch upon God, we are in the world of an infinite variety of possibles. Perhaps each reader will find among these saintly persons a particular sister-soul with whom to share some secret longing. All of them are offering us a deep and personal message.

MECHTILD, the German nun writing in the flowery language of the Courts of Love, alternates from prose to poetry and back again in dialogues and songs of exalted delight, revealing her humility and also an extensive wisdom and profound psychology. She ends her rich life by composing a moving hymn to the Mother of God and a perceptive analysis of the mystery of suffering.

HADEWYCK, the Flemish "beguine" reaches the heights and plumbs the depths of the mystical life, exposing its splendors and also its ambivalence: in an extraordinary, perceptive analysis, she distinguishes the genuine pleasures and possible dangers of a deep involvement in the supernatural. She writes as a true Lover of God, at times with the lyrical expressions of human love.

ANGELA, the Italian wife and mother, taken up by surprise to the seventh heaven in the company of her divine Lover, wails her despair at the loss of him — and spends the rest of her life meditating and writing about her marvelous experience. She completes her message with a treatise on love as it should be practiced by holy virgins.

JULIAN, the mysterious English lady, appears out of nowhere, somewhat like Melchizedek, and tells of her wondrous conversations with Christ. Her revelations are both Christocentric and Trinitarian in the most orthodox tradition of the Church. Her contributions are high praise for the human soul, a feminization of the excessively male conventional image of the Godhead, and a ringing note of hope for final justice and happiness.

JOSEFA, the fiery little Spanish victim of love, suffers the most dreadful forms of self-annihilation and participates vividly in the torments of Christ. As a victim-soul, she shares the vocation of another little one, Thérèse of Lisieux, and patiently resists the most violent satanic assaults, finally to reach the summit of mystical love.

CONCHITA, the aristocratic daughter of Mexico and happy mother of eight children, managed to live two parallel lives, as a socially engaged lady and as the secret participant in the living love of Christ. For over forty years, she kept a spiritual diary that amounted to sixty-six volumes, all of which reveal a spirituality both extraordinarily deep and perfectly orthodox.

LOUISA, the African-born daughter of Swiss Calvinist missionaries, overcomes her family's opposition and her earlier upbringing, to come home, at the age of thirty-six, in a Poor Clare convent in Jerusalem. She was only to live four more years, but in a state of almost constant intimacy with the Lord.

GABRIELLE, the pretty, successful, rich playwright and actress from France combines her active wordly life with a hidden spiritual experience of astonishing depth. At first, she doubts the divine origin of her gifts, but God reveals himself to her with such loving insistence that she is forced to surrender entirely to almost daily intimacy with the Lord.

Perhaps the major lesson to be gathered from such a variety of experiences is that *the roads to God are as many as there are individual human beings*. Nationality, social standing, education, occupation, do not count. The only important thing is openness to the Spirit of Love.

At times, as in the case of Angela, the message from beyond comes as a bolt from the blue. In other cases, there may have been long preliminary whisperings from the Spirit, heard only in the peace of a prayerful and expectant mind. The Spirit alone knows how many times he has spoken to men and women of our space age, only to be crowded out by the clamor and demands of our violent and pleasure-seeking ways.

If relatively few mystical revelations have come down to us, it may also be that most of the few who did respond to the call are unable to communicate what they have received. The number of mystically gifted people is much higher than would appear from the written records of the spiritual life.

Even an acknowledged spiritual experience may result in opposite subjective reactions. The first, and perhaps the most common, is to keep it secret because it is too deep and overwhelming to be revealed. This is generally the case with private revelations. The other reaction is to shout the news from the rooftops because it is too good to be savored alone. In some instances there is even a command to diffuse the Good News abroad.

If after reading the present book, you feel uplifted by an increase of your love for God and neighbor; if you part from it with a feeling that, for some few moments, you have been raised to the highest reaches of life; if you hunger for more and are eager to "taste and see" for yourself "how sweet the Lord is" (Ps.33:9), then the Word of God has come alive in you. May He be forever praised!

BIBLIOGRAPHY
(The following is a limited list of sources
and additional readings.)

MECHTILD OF MAGDEBURG

Mechtild's original manuscript — the six books in Middle German collected by Henry of Halle, and the seventh composed later in Helfta — have not survived. However, we do have Henry of Halle's translation into Latin (*Basle MS.*) and that of Henry of Nördlingen into High German (*Einsiedeln, 277, ff.1-165*) which seems to be closest to the original.

A critical edition of Henry of Nördlingen's translation was published under the title, *Offenbarungen der Schweister Mechtild von Magdeburg, oder Das Fliessende Licht des Gottheit* by G. Morel, Ratisbonne, 1869, and reprinted in Darmstadt in 1963 and 1976. The Latin text of Henry of Halle was published as the second volume of *Revelationes Gertrudianae et Mechtildianae* by Poitiers, Paris, 1877, edited by Paquelin. The text of Paquelin was then re-translated into German under the title *Leben und Offenbarungen der hl. Gertruda und der Schweister Mechtildis*, and published by J. Müller, Ratisbonne, 1881. A French edition, translated by Paquelin from his Poitiers edition of 1877 was then published in Paris by the same Poitiers.

See also:

Lucy Menzies: *The Revelations of Mechtild of Magdeburg*, Longmans Green, London 1953, from which present excerpts are quoted.
Sister Mary Jeremy, O.P.: *Scholars and Mystics*, Henry Regnery, Chicago, 1962 (Covering Mechtild of Hackeborn, Gertrude the Great and Mechtild of Magdeburg).
Dictionnaire de spiritualité ascétique et mystique, LXVI-LXVII, Beauchesne, Paris, 1978.

HADEWYCK OF ANTWERP

(As occurs with medieval names, there are various spellings. We have chosen the one which seems most familiar to American readers.)

Hadewyck's works in Early Flemish consist in fourteen *Visions*, many *Letters*, and a collection of rhymed *Poems*, published in a first modern edition in 1875. A critical edition appeared in 1908/1914 under the direction of Father Van Mierlo. The present excerpts of poems are translated from the original. The text from the letters is translated from the French of Edition de la Phalange listed below.

Liliane Wouters: *Bréviaire des Pays-Bas* — An anthology, XIIIth to XVth centuries — *Collection Pays-Bas, Flandres* — Editions Universitaires, Louvain, N.D.

J. Van Mierlo: *Hadewych, une mystique flamande du XIIIe siècle, Revue d'Ascétique et de Mystique,* Louvain, July/October 1924.

De Jaegher, S.J.: *Hadewych* in *Anthologie mystique,* Paris, Desclée de Brouwer, 1924.

Anthologie de la mystique des Pays-Bas with introduction by Marc Eemans, Editions de la Phalange, Brussels, 1937.

Hadewijch, Brieven, original text with modern Flemish translation, with introduction by F. Van Bladel and B. Spaapen, Lannoo, Tielt and The Hague, 1954.

Baptiste Porion: *Hadewyck,* in the collection *La vigne du Carmel,* Paris, Editions du Seuil, 1954.

Hadewijch: Poems in Middle-Flemish with modern translation, with an introduction by E. Rombauts and N. De Paepe, Tjeenk Willink, Zwolle, 1961.

Jean Orcibal: *Saint Jean de la Croix et mystiques Rheno-flamands, Collection Présence du Carmel,* Nr. 6, Bruges, Desclée de Brouwer 1966.

Hadewijch: Poems, A selection by N. De Paepe (Flemish), Ghent-Louvain, Wetenschappelijke Uitegeverij an Boekhandel, 1968.

Hadewijch: Poems, a Selection and Fundamental Study of a Middle-Flemish writer (Flemish) by N. De Paepe, Ghent-Louvain, Story-Scientia, 1968 (2 Vols.).

Hadewijch: Spiritual letters followed by the *Seven Degrees of Love,* translated into French by J.B., M.P., Geneva, Mar Tingay, 1972.

Further information on Belgian mystics may be obtained from:

— Ruusbroecgenootschap, Prinsstraat 13, B 2000, Antwerp, Belgium.

— Bibliothèque des Facultès Universitaires, Rue de Bruxelles 61, B 5000 Namur, Belgium.

For more complete texts, see *"Hadewijch, the Complete Works,"* translation and introduction by Mother Columba Hart, O.S.B., Paulist Press, Ramsey, N.J. 1980, part of the series *"The Classics of Western Spirituality."* The translations of the excerpts quoted in our work are slightly different in Mother Columba's version, and no attempt has been made there to provide a rhythmic version of the poem.

ANGELA OF FOLIGNO

The Book of the Experience of the True Faithful may be found in many manuscripts. The most reliable seem to be MS. 342 of Assisi, MS.1/141 of the Irish Monastery of St. Isidore in Rome, MS.CXII of St. Scholastica in Subiaco, MSS. 2864-71 and 2233 of the Bibliotheque Royale of Brussels, MS. 398 of Museum Bollandianum in Brussels, and MS. 1741 of the University of Bologna.

The principal published editions are:

— Latin editions in Spain: Alcala, 1502, Toledo 1505

— Latin edition in Italy: Venice, 1521

— Latin edition in France: Guillaume Chaudière, Paris, 1598, an incomplete compilation reprinted and/or re-edited in Cologne (1601), Antwerp (1643), with a French translation in Amsterdam (1696), completed by Boccolini in Foligno (1714).

Other editions in Spanish, Italian, Flemish and French were published between 1497 and 1696.

Ernest Hello published a very far from perfect but highly successful edition in Paris in 1868.

None of these texts are either satisfactory or complete.

There are two excellent editions in French:

Le livre de la bienheureuse soeur Angèle de Foligno du Tiers Ordre de Saint François, original documents edited and translated by Father Paul Doncoeur, Paris, Art Catholique, 1926.

Le livre de l' expérience des vrais fidèles par Sainte Angèle de Foligno, edited by M.J. Ferré (Latin and French texts), Paris, E. Droz, 1927.

The excerpts offered in this book are based on the Ferré text.

JULIAN OF NORWICH

The Revelations of Divine Love exist in two versions. The shorter, dated 1413, probably a first and original dictation, exists in a single copy in Latin (British Museum, MSS Additional No. 37790) which passed through the hands of a Reverend Francis Peck in the eighteenth century, was then owned by Lord Amherst, and ultimately was purchased by the British Museum in 1910.

The longer version exists in three manuscripts:

A sixteenth-century copy in Latin (Bibliothèque Nationale, Paris, Fonds Anglais No. 40, Biblioteca Bigotiana 388).

A seventeeth-century copy in middle-English (British Museum, MS Sloane 2499).

An eighteenth-century slightly modernized English version (British Museum, MS Sloane 3705).

The major difference between the two versions is that the shorter contains the essence of Julian's revelations, while the longer offers additions resulting from twenty years of religious life and the progressive development of her mystical thought.

Among the many recent editions, the following deserve to be mentioned:

Dom Roger Huddleston: *Revelations of Divine Love Shewed to a Devout Ankress, by Dame Julian of Norwich,* Newman Press, Westminster, MD, 1952.

Paul Molinari, S.J.: *Julian of Norwich: The Teaching of a Fourteenth-Century English Mystic,* Longmans Green & Co., New York, 1958.

James Walsh, S.J.: *The Revelations of Divine Love of Julian of Norwich,* Abbey Press, St. Meinrad, IN, 1974.

M.L. del Mastro: *Julian of Norwich, Revelations of Divine Love,* Image Books, NY, 1977.

Edmond Colledge & James Walsh: *A Book of Showings to the Anchoress Julian of Norwich,* Pontifical Institute of Mediaeval Studies, Toronto, 1978.

Julian of Norwich, Showings, Paulist Press, New York, 1978.

The interpretation offered in this book is our own.

JOSEFA MENENDEZ

Original notes were written in Spanish, and belong to the Society of the Sacred Heart, Madrid. A first and limited collection of excerpts was translated into French and published by *Apostolat de la Prière*, Toulouse, 1938, under the title, *Un appel à l'amour*.It was immediately followed by many translations and reprints.

In 1944, a much more complete edition (730 pp.) was published under the same title, with a running commentary, an introduction by H. Monier Vinard, S.J., and a conclusion by F. Charmot, S.J.

This in turn was translated into English and published by the Newman Press, Westminster, MD, 1949, under the title: *The Way of Divine Love, or the Message of the Sacred Heart to the World, and a Short Biography of His Messenger Sister Josefa Menéndez, Coadjutrix Sister of the Society of the Sacred Heart of Jesus, 1890-1923*.

The selection offered above is based on this version, with some corrections resulting from a comparison with the French.

CONCEPCION CABRERA DE ARMIDA (CONCHITA)

The diary of Conchita consists in sixty-six manuscript volumes. They were edited and condensed by M.M. Philipon, O.P., and translated into English by Aloysius J. Owen, S.J. *Conchita — A Mother's Spiritual Diary*, Alba House, NY, 1978.

This is the source of the excerpts offered above.

LOUISA JAQUES

The notebooks of Louisa Jaques were edited by the Very Reverend Sylvère van den Broeck, O.F.M., of St. Savior Monastery, Jerusalem, and printed in 1942 under the title: *Soeur Marie de la Trinité*.

They were translated into English and published by the Newman Press, Westminster, MD, 1950, under the title, *The Spiritual Legacy of Sister Mary of the Holy Trinity, Poor Clare of Jerusalem (1901-1942)*. This book was reprinted in 1954.

GABRIELLE BOSSIS

The diary of Gabrielle Bossis covers a period between August 22, 1936 and May 25, 1950. Some excerpts were published under a pseudonym in 1948. The book was a phenomenal success.

After Gabrielle's death in 1950, a second volume, prefaced by Daniel-Rops, revealed her identity. Three more volumes followed at the request of grateful and enthusiastic readers, then a sixth volume giving her biography and a seventh containing additional dialogue. These seven volumes, in the original French, were published by Beauchesne, Paris, under the title *Lui et Moi*.

In 1969, the Editions Paulines of Sherbrooke, Quebec, Canada, published *He and I*, a two-volume condensation translated into English by Evelyn M. Brown. This is the text we have followed, with some slight adjustments, for instance the old-fashioned capitalization of the pronouns of the Godhead has been avoided; also "thee" and "thy" have been replaced by "you" and "your."

INDEX OF PROPER NAMES

INDEX OF TOPICS

Additional publications
from **ALBA HOUSE**
on
WOMANHOOD

THE GRACE TO BE A WOMAN
by: Georgette Blaquiere

The fruit of one woman's meditations on the way the Gospels portray
Jesus as a loving liberator of the women he came in contact with,
especially in moments of crisis. The significance of these encounters is
just as vital for the women of today as it was for those who lived at the
time of Jesus.

"Inspirational, reflective, insightful! Author Blaquiere is not a women's libber nor a militant feminist. In her own words, she is 'simply
happy to be a woman,' and this joy radiates from every page of her work
. . . A male and female audience will enjoy this unique glimpse of
womanhood as Jesus saw it. Women will develop a greater awareness of
their Christian call to ministry in the faith, and men will find a remarkable
new dimension to the definition of 'woman.' "

MARRIAGE & FAMILY LIVING
"For me, both as a man and as a priest, Christ's vision of woman
which this book reveals is an inestimable gift. I hope that it will help the
women of our day sing the Magnificat of their own rediscovered feminin-
ity." *Fr. Juan-Miguel Garrigues*
"The author invites the reader to join her on a personal journey
through the New Testament as it relates to women. Blaquiere perceives a
deliberate intention by Jesus 'to restore woman to her original position —
dignified and free before God and humanity.' She presses her ear very
hard to the Gospel stories and is most successful when she unpacks layers
of meaning in key words." CATHOLIC LIBRARY WORLD   *paper* / **$6.95**